YES, YOU CAN!
LIVE YOUR DREAM

A 12-Step Complete Manual

Maria & Mats Löfkvist

AuthorHouse™
1663 Liberty Drive
Bloomington, IN 47403
www.authorhouse.com
Phone: 1 (800) 839-8640

© 2017 Maria & Mats Löfkvist. All rights reserved.

No part of this book may be reproduced, stored in a retrieval system,
or transmitted by any means without the written permission of the author.

Published by AuthorHouse   04/13/2017

ISBN: 978-1-5246-5949-3 (sc)
ISBN: 978-1-5246-5950-9 (e)

Print information available on the last page.

Any people depicted in stock imagery provided by Thinkstock are models,
and such images are being used for illustrative purposes only.
Certain stock imagery © Thinkstock.

This book is printed on acid-free paper.

Because of the dynamic nature of the Internet, any web addresses or links contained in this book may have changed since publication and may no longer be valid. The views expressed in this work are solely those of the author and do not necessarily reflect the views of the publisher, and the publisher hereby disclaims any responsibility for them.

"Simple, in-depth, clear and wise guidance to follow and then bring into fruition what you desire most in your life".
Suryo Linda Gardner, Psychotherapist MA, LMP, CBP, CBI.

"Great guidance for building capacity and character for the youth of the future, and will certainly make a change to the world".
Eliza Hunt (Film Producer)

TABLE OF CONTENTS

Acknowledgements.. vii

Introduction ix

How to use this Manual xi

1: Creating Your Dream Lab 1

2: Observe Your Thoughts and Feelings 19

3: The Unlimited Dreamer 37

4: Your Dream Intention: Believing or Knowing 49

5: Manifestation Plan - Your Dream Plan 65

6: Sending Out Your Dream 81

7: Research about Your Dream 93

8: Look for the Signs 103

9: Taking Action on the Signs 115

10: Acceptance 125

11: Be Patient and Trust 139

12: Celebrate and Give Thanks 147

Final words 159

ACKNOWLEDGEMENTS

When the student is ready, the teacher will appear.

There have been so many exceptional teachers that have crossed our path to make this book a reality. We hold our upmost respect for our parents, who have been our first and most important teachers, holding and believing in us throughout the process of life and the creation of this book.

To our teachers, our family:

Maria: To my loving and supporting husband, Guillermo, for always being there with kind words of encouragement. To our children, Mathias, Marina, Itzel and Memo, for their patience and inspiration in sharing the needs of young people of today.

Mats: To my beautiful wife and best friend Sia, for supporting all areas of my life, including my many unusual projects. To our eight children, Alofa, Miracle, Rica, Cim, Seipepa, Uiti, Rex and Leon, for their loving care for Mum and Dad.

INTRODUCTION

Who we are!

Mats: Internet marketing consultant and brave dreaming coach, former general manager for major hotel resorts, captain of large sailing yachts, and Lieutenant in the Swedish Navy.

Maria: Inspirational speaker and brave dreaming coach, registered nurse, spa designer, director and instructor for the, "Swedish School of Massage Therapy" in Mexico.

They are a brother and sister from Sweden and founders of the non-profit organization, *Global Mentor Aid*, an online mentoring program for young people.

"We grew up in Sweden, but in our early twenties we left and went onto different paths, only seeing each other at rare family occasions. Life took us on incredible journeys with vast ranges of experiences. From traditional education and traveling the world, to sailing across the Atlantic Ocean ten times and later living abroad with indigenous people for over twenty-five years each. For Mats, it was Samoa, a small island in the South Pacific, and for Maria, it was Tulum, Mexico. We lived in cultures that were extremely different from our own.

We formed our families with many children because of our love for little ones. Our lives have been filled with joy and sorrow, times of abundance and periods of scarcity. We experienced blazing sun, endless beaches, hurricanes, and tsunamis. The lessons we learned and the knowledge we obtained emerged from our authentic life experience."

Why are we doing this?

Our primary focus has always been to create and manifest our dreams, to do what we wanted in life. We made our life journey without having money, but with the trust that we could make our dream come true. We transformed this experience into a step by step manual of how to create *your* dream. We realized that if we'd had this information at a younger age, everything would have been much easier and we would have gotten to our goals more quickly. Now we want to share our experience and relevant awareness with you.

It is all about you.

We believe in **you**, and we know that you have something special to share with the world. You are here for a reason, and you are unique and perfect just as you are right now.

The clarity will come from inside of you, not from outside information.

We will take you step by step on a journey inside yourself, where **your** internal voice will guide you in which direction to take. To find the path that is right for you. We won't impose any belief on you. You will find out who you are, with all your strength and inspiration in life. We want you to treat yourself with integrity and respect, learning self-love and how to be gentle with yourself when life doesn't go your way.

Let's put it simply. We want to be your mentor, to get you on your unique path in life, which will make you happy and fulfilled, no matter what you do.

Mats & Maria

How to Use this Manual.

- Get a notebook and name it your, "**Brave Dreaming Journal.**" Make sure you always write down the exercises in your journal. Later it will become your proof that your dream is in creation.

- Our manual presents a step by step process to create your dream. Do every step in order, as each level builds on the previous step. Don't stop in the middle of the process thinking that you are clear, and start skipping the last steps. You need the whole manual to make the movements for creation into a reality. Take it in your own time; there is no pressure.
- Go back and repeat previous exercises for more clarity, if needed.
- Do all the exercises and write them down, as they are the key to opening you up to the creation of your dreams. Some of the exercises entail working on similar aspects of your dream, but each exercise is meant to take you deeper and give you more clarity, allowing yourself to see your goal from different angles.

The Purpose

When you finish this course, you will have:

- A step by step manual to create your dream.
- A handbook that you can apply to any desire and follow for the rest of your life.

Important: Before You Get Started

- We are all different, and you need to be completely open for how your dream will come to you. The experience is different for every person.
- Your dream might not manifest during the time of the course. Depending on what you want to bring into your life, it can take one day, one week, one year or maybe ten years.
- You need to continue getting clear, doing the exercises, and holding your intention and dream vision until it manifests, knowing that it will happen.

These symbols will help you to recognize the following:

 Exercises and Summary Exercise Tools.

 Writing in your Brave Dreaming Journal.

 Visualization.

 Summary of each Step.

 What you have done so far.

STEP 1

CREATING YOUR DREAM LAB

CREATING YOUR DREAM LAB

Are you ready to create your future?

You create your future whether you are aware of it or not. Now it's time to know how to do it on purpose, *intentionally*. You will learn how to dream up every part of the future you desire. You are the only person who can make and change your future, and now you will learn how to create it, as YOU like.

Everything starts with a thought, a dream.

Since you were a small child, you've always had daydreams. Your dream content might change with age, but you never stopped dreaming. Every dream starts in your mind as an imagined future. Some thoughts don't stay for long and briefly pass you by, and others are charged with feelings and desires and stay forever.

Maybe you got confused about your dream because of outside influences from parents, school, religion, and society. Once you get clear about what makes you happy, you will gain your direction.

You are the most important person right here and right now.

I bet this is new for you - to have that attention on your own importance. But the reality is, without you, the future will not be the same. In life, we often think that we don't matter and can't see how our participation can make a difference. But as time passes, as we like to tell you, it's not that way; you are precious.

You are outstanding and unique with an individual and clear purpose in life. This purpose will make you happy and give your life meaning.

We all want to be happy, but what is happiness?

Did you know that being happy has nothing to do with outer circumstances? It is an internal feeling. Happiness is attainable for all of us, at all times. Often it is a choice to be happy and to feel good. Happiness starts with your inner contentment. It is available to you independently of your finances, your health, or your living situation. You have the ability to be authentic and genuine to yourself, finding your own internal, true happiness.

Life will take you on a journey with ups and downs, triggering all possible emotions, and it's easy to get off track. When you have your toolbox of how to get back to your inner happiness and peace, it makes for a smoother ride.

Before you can have more, you need to see what you already have.

One of the tools is to count your blessings. Often, we think we don't have enough "stuff." Maybe you think you don't have enough clothing, shoes, expensive toys, electrical gadgets, telephones, computers or something else you desire. Wanting more all the time is normal. That is perfectly fine, but it is important not to forget what you already have. You can get blind to it by being so used to having it, and being so accustomed to wanting more. You might hear that your friends got something new and you are feeling that longing inside, that desire to have the same thing.

Count your blessings.

Now, we are not talking about material things like clothes or other possessions. We are talking about, *that which most matters in life.* The blessings that you were born with, the foundation of your life. It is essential to become aware of these gifts so you may begin to count them and feel gratitude.

The first blessing is that you are alive. You are here physically, and even if you are not completely healthy or your body doesn't function the way you wish, you still have many blessings.

- If you have all your body parts working, you are blessed to see with your eyes, hear with your ears, and talk with your mouth: think about how it would be to be blind, deaf or mute.
- You can move your body, walk, run, moving your arms and hands: what about if you were paralyzed?
- You can think with your brain: what if you didn't understand anything when people talked to you?
- Your heart is beating and you are breathing. Without your breath, you would not get air and oxygen to your heart, which is necessary for you to stay alive.

These things are all taken care of without you paying any attention to them. Your body is a marvelous living machine. These are blessings that you might not think about, but if you lost any of them, you certainly would. It is easy to get lost in only thinking of what you want in the material world and forget the parts that matter.

Remember the magnificence of who you are and say, **"Thank You!"**

When you feel that you don't have enough or that you are not good enough, then count your blessings one by one. I can see, I can move my body, I can smell, etc...

When it all feels dark inside, and you have lost your confidence, then remember that **one** spark of light takes away the darkness. Your blessings are the light.

*To receive more in life, first be thankful
for what you already have!*

 Exercise Tool 1: Say, Thank You!

- **In the morning,** when you wake up, start to count your blessings and say **thank you**.
- **At night,** before going to sleep, **express your thanks** for the day and remember your blessings and every small thing you received during the day.

STEP 1 | CREATING YOUR DREAM LAB

Let's start finding out more about your dream.

This first part of the course is the most important: to get clear about your dream. If you are crystal clear about what you desire, then you can do the rest.

I know what I want! Why do I need to get clear about my dream?

It is great if you already know what you want. Maybe you want to become a doctor, lawyer, nurse, engineer, pilot, singer, actor, painter or some other type of professional. Perhaps you are dreaming about traveling or having a house and family. Maybe your dream is to help nature, people and animals in the world to create a sustainable future. Once you have your dream, you need to get clear. It is one thing to have an idea of what you want, but another thing to make it clear. What is its meaning? How will you get there?

As long as your dream stays fuzzy and cloudy, it won't happen. You make it happen by clarifying it, which means **knowing all the details of what you desire**. With clarity, manifestation occurs. Your dream becomes alive and you can see it as already created. Everything will first form in your mind; then the other steps will follow.

Imagine you want to travel.

Just wanting to go on holiday won't take you anywhere. You must know exactly where you'd like to go and plan how you will get there. You will need to know where to buy a ticket, what day and time you can leave, what you need to pack for your trip, which hotel to book, what to do at the new place, and much more. Otherwise, how could you ever end up at the place you'd like to visit? Your goals and desires work the same way; the clearer you are about your dream, the easier it is to create it.

STEP 1 | CREATING YOUR DREAM LAB

You need to know what you want, to get what you want.

Why are you not already clear about your dream?

- Maybe you have never been told that you are the maker of your dreams, the creator of your future. Perhaps you have been conditioned since your upbringing not to believe in yourself. It's likely that you were affected by limiting social norms, and comments from friends, parents, and teachers who told you what to think, feel and how to behave to fit in.
- Maybe you have been taught to focus on what society wants you to do, and not to follow **your dream,** of what makes you happy.

- Maybe nobody has seen your personal abilities and strengths. Or you didn't dare to focus on them yourself, and it all got forgotten in trying to fit in and to be accepted.

Many times, we are following what other people want just to fit in and be accepted.

The benefits of getting clear and following your dream:

- You are no longer functioning in reaction to what other people think and feel about you. You follow your personal path of what makes you happy.
- You will know the exact education or knowledge needed to start in the direction of your dream. You enjoy learning whatever you need to get your dream going.
- When you are doing what you love to do, it doesn't feel like work anymore and you will enjoy every minute of it.

- People with the same interest will start approaching you and you will have the possibility to help others, which in turn helps you.
- When you are clear about what you desire, everything in life starts to work in your favor, and it will come to you.
- When you do what you love to do, you can use it to help others and easily make it into your own future business.

Obstacles to getting clear of what you desire:

Here are a few things that you might experience when you start getting clear on your dream:

- You might feel afraid it will not work out the way you want.
- You have the feeling of not fitting into your old world anymore.
- You get impatient while waiting and stop trusting in your dream.
- People who you thought would support you show a different side of themselves.
- You can feel lonely, unsupported and scared.

There could be millions of other reasons why you feel discouraged.

We know you are ready for this!

Getting clear about your dream is an exciting road to walk and remember, it is not a race. It is the actual journey, appreciating every small step, which will take you towards your dream. So, enjoy your time and **walk slowly, don't run.**

Just to clarify!

When we are talking about your dream, this doesn't mean that you can only have one dream. You can, of course, have as many dreams as you like, big and small, in many different areas of your life. When you do the exercises, it is recommended to work on one dream at a time.

Before we take you into your dream lab, let's make sure you enter with what is right for you.

 Exercise Tool 2: **What makes you feel happy right now?**

Close your eyes and be still in your body.

Breathe deeply and start to think about;

- Something you would love to do or have right now.
- Something that you are longing for and it would make you completely happy.
- Let your mind make up anything you desire!

Open your eyes and finish the questions and write down the **first five** things that come to your mind. Don't judge whether it is possible or not.

1: I would be totally happy if I had or could do…
2: I would be totally happy if I had or could do…
3: I would be totally happy if I had or could do…
4: I would be totally happy if I had or could do…
5: I would be totally happy if I had or could do…

Look at the above statements and feel the significance they have in your life right now.

Ask yourself:

If I could only have one of these five statements, which would that be?

Look at your five statements of what makes you completely happy and feel the one that is most important to you at this time in your life. Take this statement out and make it your "number one."

Then continue with the following four statements and ask the same question again.

If I could only have one of these four statements, which would that be?

Do this over and over until you have a sequence from 1 to 5 of what makes you happy right now.

Write down in your **Brave Dreaming Journal** the question:
What makes me feel happy right now? Followed by your five answers.

With these five answers vividly situated in your mind, enter into the dream lab to explore them in more detail and make them into your dream.

Exercise Tool 3: Making your Dream Lab.

 3:1 Visualization.
(Please read through the exercise once before you start)

Relax: Make yourself comfortable. Sit or lay down, close your eyes and keep them closed during the whole exercise. Take some deep breaths to relax your entire body. Relax all parts starting with your feet. Relax all the way up through your legs, your back, arms, head, and face. Relax your mind and let go of the thoughts you have.

Dream Lab Key: You are now going to create your dream lab. Imagine that you have the key in your hand to your private space, where you can do anything you want, your personal dream lab. Open the door and step into the most creative and peaceful place where your mind can be entirely free to make up anything you want.

Where are you? Your dream lab could be at any location you like, in the jungle, on the beach, on a mountain, in your bedroom, or at any other peaceful place. Take your time to see the place, smell it, feel it, look at the colors around you. Can you hear anything? What sound is there? Look at where you are.

How do you feel? Take a deep breath and pay attention to how you feel inside. Enjoy your time and get deep into the feeling of being totally free, limitless and happy. There are no fears, no worries, and no obstacles. The dream lab is your safe and secure place where you can feel good and create any future dream that you want.

STEP 1 | CREATING YOUR DREAM LAB

Remember what makes you happy: See it in front of you. Let your imagination run wild making it up just the way you want. See what makes you happy and make it into a dream. See it as vividly as possible, pay attention to all the small details. What do you do? Where are you? How does it make you feel? Stay with it for as long as you like.

Come back: When you are ready, take some deep breaths and imagine that you walk back again, towards the door. Before you leave, turn around and take a good look at your beautiful dream lab. A place of peace and creativeness, where you can come back anytime.

With your dream and all the great feelings fresh in your mind, you walk out the door, and you lock it with your key. Only you have the key to your dream lab. Take another deep breath and start to come back, feel your body and open your eyes. Stretch yourself and continue with the following exercise.

3:2 Writing about your dream.

Describe your dream in your **Brave Dreaming Journal** as detailed as possible with all your positive and strong feelings.

Write the answers to these following questions:

1. Where were you?
2. What did you experience in your dream?
3. How did it make you feel?

 Exercise Tool 4: Look at your dream continually.

- Keep your **dream vivid.** Look at it and feel it as many times as possible and remind yourself of it before you go to sleep at night.

    Go back into the dream lab and make changes, adjustments, and freely add or take away parts. Make your dream clearer every time and write down all the details in your **Brave Dreaming Journal** whenever you come back.

STEP 1 | CREATING YOUR DREAM LAB

I have many dreams, what do I do?

If you have many dreams that you want to manifest, you still have to take just one at the time into the "dream lab." If not, your mind will fluctuate in between different dreams, and you won't get clear on any of them. Decide on one dream, and let the mind create the details.

Know that you are creating your life every day by holding onto your dream. Start to become aware of it, letting your dream form your future.

You create your dream. Become a brave dreamer.

 Summary:

- You have made your dream lab.
- You have started to get clear on what you desire.
- You have lived your dream in your mind.

 Summary Exercise Tools:

1   Say Thank You!
2   What makes you feel happy right now?
3:1 Visualization - Making your Dream Lab.
3:2 Writing about your dream.
4   Looking at your dream continually.

What you have done so far:

Step 1: You have made your dream lab.

STEP 2

OBSERVE YOUR THOUGHTS AND FEELINGS

OBSERVE YOUR THOUGHTS AND FEELINGS

Did you know that your thoughts and feelings are the real creators of your life? Now let's get right into finding out how they create and affect your *dream*.

The thoughts that you keep in your mind and think over and over will slowly take a form and become your reality.

The feelings that you hold inside are the fuel to empower your thoughts. The stronger the feelings you add to your thoughts, the faster your mind will begin to manifest your dream.

Thoughts and feelings work in both positive and negative directions.

For example: If you want a new phone but you feel you can't get one. Everyone else around you has a new phone. But you're convinced that it would be impossible for you to get one, so then most likely you will not get it.

But...

What if you want a new phone and you feel worthy of having one? You feel it with certainty and passion throughout your whole body. Sooner or later your mind will find a way to get it.

Why is it like that?

Because you need to have **your thoughts and feelings saying and wanting the same thing** for your dream to happen. It is vital to become aware of what is going on inside of yourself; not just hoping, wishing and thinking you know what you want.

Be clear of the messages that both the thoughts and the feelings are telling you. It must be the same message from both of them. Most of the time you think you know what you want, but it is only once you start to observe your thoughts and feelings that it will become evident.

Strong negative feelings and worries will create more negativity and fears.

These feelings will not take you to where you want to go. They will only produce more of its kind. It's okay to feel anxious; it can be a natural reaction to situations in life. It is the constant negative feelings and worries that create the negative result.

Focus on what you desire and not on what you don't desire.

Feelings and thoughts have to want the same thing.
You can't think feelings!
You feel feelings, and you think thoughts.

Well, that sounds obvious! But it isn't. I bet you are often *thinking* your feelings instead of *feeling* them. For instance; when you like the bullied girl or boy but ignore them from fear of getting bullied yourself. You may start to think like the "cool" people just to be accepted. Or you'd like to help the bullied classmate in the corner, but from fear of standing out, you just stand there doing nothing. You are thinking one thing and feeling another.

Are you feeling your feelings or thinking your feelings?

When you take action out of habit, you are usually thinking your feelings instead of feeling them. It's ok and totally normal because maybe no one has ever told you how to see the difference between your thoughts and your feelings. Honestly, very few people in the world have learned this. Now you have the chance to become aware of it.

Let's have a closer look at the difference between a thought and a feeling:

Observe what you are thinking.

Start to observe what you are thinking related to your dream. Since your thoughts create the reality through your mind, you first have to find out what you are thinking. You have thousands of thoughts going through your head every day. Most of them are made up from:

- How you think about life, related to your previous experiences.
- Your present situation.
- What you have learned from society.
- Your dream about the future.

Most of your thoughts are recurrent, which means that the same thoughts come back again and again but with different words.

Common recurrent thoughts include:

Scarcity thoughts: I can't have it. It is too expensive. I am not worthy of it. They can have it but not me. I wish I could have it. It is impossible. I am too poor.

Fearful thoughts: I tried, but it didn't work. I can't do it. I don't have the time. Easy for you to say, but I can't. I don't know how to do it. It is too difficult. I am not intelligent enough.

Lack of self-esteem thoughts: Nobody loves me. I am always alone. I always lose. Nobody understands me. I have no friends. Nobody likes me. I am too shy. I always make mistakes.

Become aware of your negative thoughts: You probably have no idea what kind of thoughts are recurring in your mind. The thoughts go on automatically. When you first start to observe your thoughts, then you are able to see them clearly, as well as the effects they have on you.

- Negative thoughts will hurt you and bring you away from your dream. When you become aware of what you are thinking, you can **catch yourself** having those negative thoughts.
- Catching yourself doesn't mean that you are changing your thoughts, but you will **become aware** of them. You just know that you have negative thoughts, and you know what they tell you.
- **Don't judge** yourself or analyze where the thoughts come from, **just observe them**.

Observing your thoughts will change them.

Being aware of your thoughts changes them. There's nothing more you need to do other than being constantly aware of your unwanted thoughts. It is like turning on the light in a dark room, the darkness disappears on its own. The darkness just doesn't exist anymore. When you are consistently aware of your negative thoughts, they change on their own. Don't fight them or try to change them, just learn to observe them. That is how your negative thoughts will go away.

It might sound too easy or simple, but this is how it works. Start to train your mind to remember to observe your thoughts. The mind is easily distracted and wants to do what it has always done, so it takes an effort to begin watching and becoming aware. It is not enough to just do it once or twice; you need to do it continuously to catch your negative thoughts.

Focus your energy on STAYING AWARE of your thoughts and NOT on trying to change them.

Practice observing what you are thinking to become aware of it. Never judge if it's right or wrong, just listen and find out what your thoughts are telling you.

STEP 2 | OBSERVE YOUR THOUGHTS AND FEELINGS

 Exercise Tool 1: Listen to your thoughts.
(Read through the exercise before you start)

A miniature you. Imagine that you shrink yourself down to a tiny figure, sitting on your shoulder listening to your thoughts.

Listen to your thoughts. Take some deep breaths and relax. Close your eyes and just let yourself be. At first, the thoughts might try to trick you by being quiet. Have patience and be still and continue to observe. The more you relax, the more the thoughts will run wild. Thoughts are quickly jumping from here to there. It is easy to get carried away or distracted and forget to be the observer.

Practice staying present and observe the thoughts for 2 minutes. If you find this difficult, say out loud every thought that comes to your mind for one minute. Yes! You will then hear all that comes out!

Listen to your mind chatter. Listen within to your inner conversation and realize that this mind chatter talks all the time in your head, even when you try to concentrate on other things. These thoughts go on and on unconsciously, even if you don't listen to them, but they sure can be distracting.

Your Feelings Determine Your Life.

Observe what you are <u>feeling.</u>

Feelings work in a similar way to your thoughts; they affect you unconsciously.

Did you know that all decisions are feeling based? First, comes a feeling that creates a thought, which in turn might create another feeling. All of this happens so fast that you won't know what comes first, the feeling or the thought.

For example: When meeting a new person, in the first ten seconds you have decided if you like him/her, making up a list of things about who you believe this person to be.

First, comes a feeling; ***Wow Yes!!! (liking)***
That creates a thought; ***I like him/her.***
That creates a new feeling; I ***feel shy.***

Observing your feelings will change them.

- When you watch the feelings connected to your thoughts about your dream, you will start to see where you have hang-ups and fears. These will determine whether or not you reach your desired goal.

- When you observe your feelings, you might find feelings that you had no idea existed inside, like anger, irritation, regrets, resentment, sadness, loss, pain, shame, guilt, jealousy, envy, fear, happiness, joy, contentment, excitement, ecstasy, etc...

- Don't try to fake it, thinking that your feelings don't exist, hoping they would be different. It is all perfect as it is, just accept whatever feelings you have.

- It is crucial to be honest with yourself and to become aware of the feelings you hold about your dream for your dream to become real.

- Again, it is your honest awareness and observation of your feelings that will change them. **Do not** attempt to change them by trying to feel different. So, don't judge or try to correct your feelings. Be very honest and start to observe your unwanted feelings continuously, and they will change on their own.

Only what you are aware of can be altered. By being conscious of the thoughts and feelings that don't serve you, they will change on their own.

Here is an example: Let's say you want to become a doctor and earn a good amount of money by helping many people. At the same time, you have a negative feeling inside because you believe that money is evil and it makes you a bad person for receiving it (which is of course not true).

If you are not aware of this negative feeling, you will probably become a doctor but work for free and never feel worthy of receiving money. It will always stop you from earning money and having the life you desire.

Becoming aware of your feelings is critical. Just like everyone else, you have a storage of negative feelings inside. Start to observe them now. When you become aware of them, don't judge them, just observe them, and they will slowly dissolve by themselves.

STEP 2 | OBSERVE YOUR THOUGHTS AND FEELINGS

When you have a clear thought or dream in combination with a strong positive feeling, you have all you need to create it. In fact, it's already created. It's only a matter of time before it will show up.

Again, your feelings give the fuel and the power to your thoughts. The more positive and happy feelings you can add to your dream, the faster it will manifest.

Exercise Tool 2: Observing Your Thoughts and Feelings.

 2:1 Visualization.

(Read through the exercise before you start. First listen to the thoughts, then to the feelings. Don't mix them, take one at the time).

Relax.

Sit or lie down, close your eyes and keep them closed during the whole visualization. Take some deep breaths to relax your entire body. Relax all parts starting with your feet. Relax all the way up through your legs, your back, arms, head, and face. Relax your mind and let go of any sticky thoughts.

Go into your dream lab.

>Bring your key and go back into your dream lab.
>Once you open the door, look around inside. Is it different today?
>Watch if there is anything new, listen to the sounds.
>Start to let the feelings of safety and relaxation come back to you.
>Find your favorite place inside, relax and bring up your dream in your mind.
>Look at it and while you see all the details, start to listen to your mind.
>Listen and observe, don't try to change anything.

Relax and watch your thoughts.

Are there any negative thoughts connected to your dream?

Maybe thoughts like:

> I don't have the money to get what I want.
> They won't let me do what I want.
> I am not good enough; I don't know how to do it.
> They can do it, but I can't.
> *Just listen and observe, don't change anything.*

Relax and watch your feelings.

After watching your thoughts, pay attention to the feelings connected to your dream. What are the feelings telling you? Feel and listen.

Maybe feelings like:

> Who will take care of everyone if I do what I want?
> I can't support myself.
> They will laugh and ridicule me.
> No one believes in me.

Just listen and observe; don't change anything.

Give thanks.

Give thanks to your thoughts and feelings for letting you know about them. Treat them with love, like scared little children inside of you.

Come back.

Take a deep breath and in your visualization, walk back towards the door. Before you leave, turn around and view your beautiful dream lab. Remember all the wonderful feelings of love, peace and safety this place gives you. Walk out and lock the door from the outside. You are the key holder and this is your secret place.

Take a deep breath, come back into the here and now by starting to feel your hands and feet, and slowly open your eyes. Come back to being completely awake.

STEP 2 | OBSERVE YOUR THOUGHTS AND FEELINGS

 2:2 Writing.

- Start to write in your **Brave Dreaming Journal** what your thoughts and feelings were telling you. Get clarity if there are any things inside of you that are stopping you from reaching your dream.
- As you write down your thoughts and feelings, read them out loud and look at them as scared children.

What would you do with a frightened child? You hold them and love them. Don't fight, judge or try to change them; they will change just by being loved and observed.

Repetition trains you to become aware.

- Repeat this exercise as many times as possible to practice being present watching your thoughts and feelings. You will then become aware of the real, *underlying mind shatter* and fear that keep you stuck.
- Remember to write everything down after each time you do the exercise. Your mind will trick you into forgetting your dream or tell you that your dream is impossible. If you ever get discouraged by somebody who doesn't believe in what you desire, you need your Brave Dreaming Journal as a reminder that your dream is real for you.

Exercise Tool 3: **Draw your dream symbol.**

- Make your secret symbol that represents your dream and reminds you of it. It can be anything like a star, flower, geometrical symbol or anything else.
- Draw this in your brave dreaming journal, put it on the wall, draw it in your hand or in any place where you regularly see it.
- This symbol will remind you of your dream every time you look at it and give you strength, courage, and trust that you are on your way towards it.

Summary:

- You are becoming aware of the thoughts and feelings you have inside.
- You are observing your thoughts and feelings related to your dream.
- You made a special symbol reminding yourself of your dream.

Summary Exercise Tools:

1   Listen to your thoughts.
2   Observing your thoughts and feelings.
2:1   Visualization
2:2   Writing
3   Draw your dream symbol.

STEP 2 | OBSERVE YOUR THOUGHTS AND FEELINGS

 What you have done so far:

Step 1: You have made your dream lab.
Step 2: You are observing your thoughts and feelings.

STEP 3

THE UNLIMITED DREAMER

The Unlimited Dreamer

It's great that you are determined to continue to get to know yourself and to reach your dream. You are on your way to creating the future you desire, and we are excited for you.

Now, it's time to get into the details of shaping your dream into something much greater. Something that you might not even believe you can have at this point in life. Now you will connect with your unlimited dreamer.

Ask yourself the question:

What would I do if I had unlimited time and money?

You can dream up anything you like;

> without any limits,
> without thinking if it would be possible or not,
> without thinking if you will have the money to do it or not,
> without any fear,
> without anyone stopping you,
> with all the time and money that you need and want.

What would your dream look like?

Your Unlimited Dream.

It doesn't matter what you are dreaming about, as long as you **love doing it, having it and being it**. It could be anything from studying, painting, writing, reading, filming, cooking, walking, talking, gardening, sports, selling, buying, hugging people, to any other thing that makes you feel happy and fulfilled.

Inspiration and passion fuel your dream.

When you do what you love to do, you get so inspired that you frequently lose track of time. You get totally absorbed and you want to do it over and over until you reach your perfection. You don't feel like you have to give up anything since it gives you such a feeling of meaningfulness, complete harmony, and passion. You just can't stop doing it.

It's time to go deeper and look closer at what makes you happy.

STEP 3 | THE UNLIMITED DREAMER

 Exercise Tool 1: **Finding out what you love to do.**

Ask yourself the following questions and **feel the answers.**

What do I love to do?

- Something that fills me with happiness
- Something that gives me joy and passion
- Something I have a real interest in
- Something that is so easy for me that I lose all sense of time doing it
- Something I keep myself updated on because it is so exciting and fun
- I would do this all the time if I had more time and money
- I am totally inspired

What would that be for you?

 Write it down in your **Brave Dreaming Journal.**

Exercise Tool 2: Be the unlimited dreamer

 Exercise Tool 2:1 Visualization

(Please read through the exercise once before you start.)

Go back to your dream lab bringing in all the things you love to do along with the good feelings they give you. Use them all to make your dream bigger.

Relax: Take a moment to relax. Close your eyes and see yourself in your dream lab being completely unlimited with time and money. Allow your mind to create the dream with what you love to do. Using all your internal strength, abilities and talents.

Dream Bigger: Feel it inside and trust yourself. Know that anything is possible and that you are truly unlimited, so allow yourself to **dream bigger than before.** Be free, and dream about what seems impossible.

Remember, you are the creator of your life. Know that you are worthy of having what you want and that it is all possible. **You can have it, you can be it, and you can do it.** Trust yourself.

Come Back: Stay with your dream and explore it for as long as you like. When you are ready, take a deep breath and come back.

Write down all the details as vividly as possible into your **Brave Dreaming Journal**. Remember, you are the unlimited dreamer, make your dream as big as you possibly can.

STEP 3 | THE UNLIMITED DREAMER

Your Dream and the Future You.

 Exercise Tool 3: **How will your life be in 10 years from now?**

Let's imagine that you are ten years older than now. Take your dream and your visions and imagine how your life will be when you have unlimited money and you can choose to do anything with your time. Let your mind run wild connecting with your inspiration and passion.

Answer the questions:

- Where do you live?
- How do you live?
- With whom do you live?
- How do you dress?
- What do you eat?
- What are you doing in a typical day?
- What education do you have?
- What kind of work are you doing?
- How does it feel to be completely happy and content with your life?
- How does it feel to have unlimited money?
- How does it feel to have unlimited time and always be doing what you want?
- What are you doing with the extra money and time that you can't use for yourself?

Write down every detail that you envision for the future in your **Brave Dreaming Journal** as if you already have it now.

Example: I am a teacher, I work in a big school with a lot of children. I dress in a jacket and tie. My day looks like… I feel like...

Example: I am the boss of my own company, dressing in a relaxed way, eating healthy foods. My day looks like...I feel like...

Obstacles Inside of You.

To follow the dream that makes you happy can sometimes feel unrealistic. The mind will try with every possible argument to tell you why you can't have your dream, and most of those arguments are fear based. This mind chatter and these beliefs can become your obstacles and you need a way to overcome them.

The future is a threat for your mind. Your conscious mind only knows your past experiences and cannot understand the future. It will do anything to keep you where you are, comfortable and safe. The saying, "***You know what you have, but you don't know what you might get***" is meant to keep you where you are and fearful of making changes.

When you live your life the same way every day and never question why you do and say things the way you do, the mind feels safe and secure. Then life goes on autopilot, repeating itself and all the things you have learned to accept. Nothing changes and life will continue to stay the same.

STEP 3 | THE UNLIMITED DREAMER

Your conscious mind (ego) only knows what happened to you in the past. The future is a threat and the ego will try to keep you safe and away from it by **not** allowing you to do anything new.

Be brave to overcome the obstacles.

To live your dream, you must be brave and do what you and other people think is scary and uncomfortable. It doesn't mean taking dangerous risks. To be brave is to take action while walking towards your dream, even if you feel scared doing it. That is how you will overcome the obstacles.

YES, YOU CAN!

Sometimes people will not understand. They might think that you've lost your mind because they never had dreams like you have. You must do what other people consider to be scary to be able to follow and reach your dream.

**If you know exactly where you want to go,
you will get to the place you want to be.**

45

STEP 3 | THE UNLIMITED DREAMER

Create Your Dream Statement.

Now you are ready to make the first dream statement. It is a short description of what you desire, your dream. It is a personal definition about the content of your dream. We will come back to this more in detail later and you will change your dream statement many times during this course. But for now, you will create your first short statement.

 Exercise Tool 4: **Create your short dream statement**.

Write down in your **Brave Dreaming Journal** a short sentence defining what is your dream. Write your statement like you already have it; I am…, I have… etc.

Examples: I am a pilot, traveling the world. I have my private red house on the beach.

Fill in the blank below.

My Dream Statement is: _____

_____

I have patience and trust that my inspiration and passion are making my dream statement come true, even if I don't know how and when. Yet!

Congratulations!
You are a huge step closer to your dream - you have defined it.

46

It's time to take yourself to the next level!

Although you already have information that very few people know and understand, it's still only the beginning of a much deeper knowledge that will change the way you live your life. From now on, you will start to create and bring your dream into reality in an active and conscious way.

Summary:

- You connected with the unlimited you through answering the question:
  What would your dream look like if you had unlimited time and money?
- You looked into obstacles to your dream.
- You found what you love to do.
- You made your dream statement.

Summary Exercise Tools:

1 Finding out what you love to do.
2 Be the unlimited dreamer.
3 How will your life be in 10 years from now?
4 Create your dream statement.

STEP 3 | THE UNLIMITED DREAMER

 What you have done so far:

Step 1: You have made your dream lab.
Step 2: You are becoming aware of your thoughts and feelings.
Step 3: You are defining your dream with unlimited time and money.

STEP 4

YOUR DREAM INTENTION: BELIEVING OR KNOWING

YOUR DREAM INTENTION: BELIEVING OR KNOWING.

Your dream is your direction, your compass.

Your dream is the guide that gives you direction in your life. It is like your personal compass. You need to know in which direction you are going to get where you want to go. If you don't have a direction, you will aimlessly float around being prone to pick up the direction of someone else so you can float together. But then it isn't your dream anymore.

What if you want to become a singer and your best friend wants to be a pilot? She talks about it all day long with intensity and passion. Then you might think that *you* want to become a pilot. Maybe you feel like your dream isn't as important as your friend's dream. It can make you insecure, and you lose your confidence, even to the point that you can feel shy talking about your dream.

Don't worry; this is normal, but it is NOT okay for you. There isn't any dream that is better or less good. All dreams are great dreams, as long as you dream. If you listen too much to your friend's dream, you will just get confused about your own.

You need to have a reliable, stable compass showing you the way to what feels right for you. We are all different and you are unique in your own way, with your special talents and personal gifts. That is why you need to hold on to your dream.

It is not important WHAT you dream of, but dreaming in itself is vital.

"Be Yourself - Everyone Else is Taken."
Oscar Wilde

Being without any dream or direction makes you feel confused and alone. If you are jumping from dream to dream in your head, not knowing what to settle for, you start to depend even more on what your friends are dreaming of and losing sight of your inner compass.

If you feel like you don't know where you are going with your life and that everybody else seems to know, don't worry!

Just continue to work through this manual and don't lose focus. You will become clearer all the time, which will take you out of the confusion.

STEP 4 | YOUR DREAM INTENTION: BELIEVING OR KNOWING

*Your dream, charged with strong feelings and emotions, is your compass, showing you which way to go. To be successful, happy and fulfilled, you must follow **Your Dream** instead of going where other people want you to go.*

Let's continue to explore what makes you unique.

You were born with unique talents, your special gifts, and passion. You have had these gifts for your whole life, but maybe you've never seen them or never were recognized for them. If you go deep down inside yourself, you **know** there is something that makes you different from the rest. It could be that you are skilled at working with your hands, that you have a very sharp mind and memory, that you are a loving, caring person, or talented at public speaking, music, singing, sport or anything else. Deeply hidden inside yourself, you know what it is, and we are going to highlight it and then base your dream on it.

Maybe you say, *"I don't know what that is, I have nothing special inside of me."*

Well! That is what **you** think, but I bet that you do, because we all do...

You were born with your unique talent and you came here to share it with all other people in this lifetime. You are not a mistake. You are hugely important to the whole. The rest of the world needs you and you need to find that special talent that you excel at, and then express it.

Let's begin to find your talent through the deeper feeling you get from your dream, which is your dream intention. This deeper feeling will point you towards your talent and also answer the question **why** you want your dream. So, let's become detectives!

Bring up your dream and hold it in your mind.
Ask yourself, *what feeling will this dream fulfill deep inside of me?*

- Feeling good when helping others.
- Feeling the need to spread an important message in the world.
- Making someone happy.
- Experiencing pure happiness for yourself.
- Feeling that you are making a difference in the world.
- Freeing yourself from worries.
Or any other feeling.

Sometimes it is something much deeper than you initially thought.

Many times, our passion serves as a gateway to understanding what your intention is. You can feel passionate about several things, but there might be one thing that stands out as more important. The passion is the powerful feeling that comes from inside and is special to you. It serves as your magnet, attracting what you desire.

Your Intention, Your Passion-Magnet.

Your deeper feeling as to **WHY** you want your dream is your intention. This heartfelt passion-magnet is not about thinking it's a good idea to help people or to do good deeds in life. **Your intention is a deeper feeling inside.**

The dream intention is your passionate internal drive, moving your energy in the direction of what you desire. It is like a strong magnet. When the passion fills your body, mind and spirit, the dream will come to you just as being drawn to a magnet. You will start to attract the right people and circumstances to accomplish your dream. That is how your intention serves as your magnet for your dream to become real.

Now, can you see why it is important to be crystal clear on WHY you want your dream, to be able to attract what you desire?

YES, YOU CAN!

Your strong intention magnet attracts the right people and circumstances to accomplish your dream.

Example: If you want to become a doctor, start to see yourself being a doctor. Watch the people you will treat, their happy faces and thankfulness as you assist them. Feel it in your whole body, how content, happy and grateful you are because you can help them. Your mind will identify with the thoughts and feelings of already being a doctor, and it will **KNOW** it to be real. Your mind doesn't know the difference between a dream and reality; they are both real.

STEP 4 | YOUR DREAM INTENTION: BELIEVING OR KNOWING

💭 **Exercise Tool 1:1** **Find your dream intention.**

Find out what feeling your dream will fulfill deep inside of you.

If you close your eyes, you can start to feel the intention moving inside of you. Sense all the cells in your body wanting it and your strong urge to express it. You get passionate thinking about it, feeling happy and expansive in your whole body. You love it so intensely that you will do it without anybody telling you. It brings you joy and happiness every time you do it or think about it.

What is your dream intention, the answer to why you want to express your unique talent?

*My dream intention (the why) is:*_____.

 Exercise Tool 1:2 **Why is this important for me?**

Take the dream intention and ask yourself,

Why is this important for me?

> *Example:*
> *Intention feeling: I like to help people when I am a doctor.*
> *Answer: Why is this important for me? It makes me happy.*

56

Take your answer and ask the question again;

Why is this important for me?

> *Example:*
> Answer: Why is this important for me? When I am happy, I feel I can do anything.

Take your answer and ask the question again;

Why is this important for me?

> *Example:*
> Answer: Why is this important for me? When I feel I can do anything, I feel no fear.

Do this five (5) times to dig deep down into yourself, getting clear on what matters to you.

 Write it down in your **Brave Dreaming Journal**.

Do you believe, or do you know your dream will come true?

Believing: A belief is something where **doubt exists;** you don't know if it is true or not. You hope that your dream will be real, but there are doubts and behind each doubt is fear. You need to go back to Step 2 and observe your thoughts and feelings, find the fear, and watch it again to get clear. Words are very powerful; be careful of how you use them. When you use the word "believe," you will most likely not gain achievement.

Knowing: When you feel you know something, there is **a real determination** inside. When you know your dream will happen, you know it is already real and done. You clearly feel it and you **have no doubts at all**. You know your dream is right for you without understanding why or how it will happen.

To illustrate the difference in feeling:

You don't believe that the sun will rise in the morning - you know it will.

Please remove **believe**, **hope** and **wish** from your vocabulary. These words only bring you more believing, hoping and wishing for, and not what you truly desire.

*When **believing** you can have something, you are telling yourself that you are **not sure** you can have it. You just **hope** or **wish** it will happen. It only creates more believing, hoping and wishing. When you **KNOW** from deep inside that you can have it, then there are no more doubts - you just know it to be true.*

STEP 4 | YOUR DREAM INTENTION: BELIEVING OR KNOWING

When KNOWING your dream is real:

- You already ARE what you want.
- You already HAVE what you want.
- You are already DOING what you want.

For example: When you know you already are a pilot, in your mind you can see the blue colored uniform and feel it on your body. You can see the cockpit and feel all the buttons and you know how each one works. You can see the runway and feel the acceleration in your whole body at takeoff. You feel the excitement of visiting new countries and the self-gratitude of making your dream come true.

 Exercise Tool 2: **Knowing or Believing About Your Dream.**

Let's take a close look at your dream to find out which part you **believe** will happen and which part you **know** will happen.

Make your list from the answers you wrote in Step 3, Exercise 3.

- Be relaxed when you do it and trust in your first feeling.
- If you have more than one dream, work with one at a time.
- Hold on to your dream intention (the reason **why** you want your dream).
- Be very honest with yourself when you ask:

Do I believe this (not sure)? Or do I know this will become real?

I Believe
Example:
I can be a doctor
I can buy a house

I Know
Example:
I will get the grades I need in school
I will get a job

 Write the whole list in your **Brave Dreaming Journal**.

 Exercise Tool 3: **Taking what you believe back to the second step.**

When you find many **beliefs** in your dream, you have doubts that it will happen. It's okay, but it's important to explore any negative thoughts and feelings connected to your dream, otherwise it cannot manifest.

Go back to the exercise in Step 2 and observe your thoughts and feelings about each of your beliefs, one by one.

When there are no more negative thoughts and feelings attached to the dream, you will start to feel that you know it will happen.

When you find more fears, it doesn't mean that you are doing anything wrong. Remember, this is a process and the deeper you go, the more fears and doubts might appear. All of us have tons of fears and they show up in different ways the deeper we go. Think of it as the layers of an onion. You are just starting to peel off the first layer.

The Two Questions Never to be Asked.

HOW will my dream happen?

You don't know how it will happen. You just won't know. Life is a bundle of coincidences, opportunities, and situations that we cannot foresee. We all live in a co-existence with other people, animals, nature and forces that we can't control. Your **intention** will draw the opportunities to you to make your dream manifest. Take one step at a time towards your goal, and as you do, the next step will appear one way or another. Life makes magic coincidences happen with people and opportunities showing up on their own when they are supposed to, and when you are ready for it. Just hold on to your dream intention and trust that it will happen, even if you don't know how.

WHEN will my dream happen?

You have no idea when it will happen. You can desire your dream to come through in a particular time frame, but in reality, you won't know when it will happen. You just have to hold your dream intention continually and trust that when the time is right, it will appear.

WHEN is the time right? You won't know because you can't know all the circumstances around your dream. Don't put a time limit to your dream; you only set yourself up for a disappointment. Take steps to get you closer to your dream, and never give up on your intention.

- Just **know** it will happen, hold on to your intention in your dream.
- Trust that the next step **will** appear once you take the first.
- Be a brave dreamer.
- **You can do it!**

 Summary:

- You got clear on your dream intention, the deeper question of **why** you want your dream.
- You checked if you truly **believe** or **know** your dream will happen, and identified whether you need to do more clarifying.
- You understand not to ask the two questions of **how** and **when** your dream will happen.

 Summary Exercise Tools:

1:1 Find your dream intention.
1:2 Why is this important for me?
2   Knowing or believing about your dream.
3   Taking what you "believe" back to the second step.

STEP 4 | YOUR DREAM INTENTION: BELIEVING OR KNOWING

 What you have done so far:

Step 1: You have made your dream lab.
Step 2: You are becoming aware of your thoughts and feelings.
Step 3: You are defining your dream with unlimited time and money.
Step 4: You are finding your intention and what you believe or know about your dream.

STEP 5

MANIFESTATION PLAN – YOUR DREAM PLAN

STEP 5 | MANIFESTATION PLAN - YOUR DREAM PLAN

Manifestation Plan - Your Dream Plan

How to Manifest Your Dream Faster.

Now it is time to put your dream on paper and write it into your manifestation plan. You will use this manifestation plan all the time, to remind yourself of your dream in a concise form, to get a better understanding of it.

Magic is happening when you put your dream on paper and create a plan. To make the most use of your manifestation plan, connect with your happy feelings and your dream intention. When you use all of your senses - looking, touching, smelling, hearing and tasting - you engage all parts of your mind and feelings. These will later inform your brain to make a picture of your dream. It is important that you stay in tune with your emotions. When you get hold of the feeling that your dream will give you, and keep that vision, your dream starts to manifest much faster.

Example: Engage all your senses - You want to eat a chocolate cookie. Close your eyes and imagine that you see a big, fat cookie full of chocolate chunks. Smell their newly baked aroma as they come out of the oven, touch and hold a hot cookie in your hand. Hear the crunch when you take the first bite; you salivate when you taste the chocolate melting in your mouth. Feel your happiness from enjoying every part of the cookie until you eat it all, and you want another one. Even feel the thirst from the sugar after you've finished.

To manifest your dream quickly, you need the same clarity, using all your senses and feelings. So, let's start!

How to Work the Manifestation Plan.

Follow the instructions below. You can write as many dreams as you like. There will be some that are short-term dreams, which are easy to reach, and others will be long term life dreams that you will reach further down the road when the time is right.

Start with the most important dream, the one you already made up in your dream lab. Try to be as clear as possible and write in short sentences. Capture the strong feelings you have for your dream, knowing that your dream is on its way.

STEP 5 | MANIFESTATION PLAN - YOUR DREAM PLAN

 Exercise Tool 1: **The Manifestation Plan.**

Download Word Document: http://www.bravedreaming.com/manifestation-plan/

 Write the answers in your **Brave Dreaming Journal.**

YES, YOU CAN!

THE MANIFESTATION PLAN

A. Describe your dream as if you have already manifested it:

B. How important is your dream? One the lowest - Ten the highest. Circle your choice.

1   2   3   4   5   6   7   8   9   10

C. Dream Intention, the deeper meaning for you and the emotional reasons why:

-

-

-

D. Benefits that you and the world will receive from your dream (one or many):

E. The Actions between where you are now and where you want to go. Actions you think will happen on your way to reaching your dream. Be creative and think outside the usual. Write as many as you like:

-
-
-
-
-
-

F. Giving Thanks: Write with emotions how grateful you are for already having achieved your dream:

G. How you will celebrate yourself? What will you do to acknowledge your progress?

Copyright Maria & Mats Löfkvist

Does your dream answer the question,

What would I love to do if I had unlimited time and money?

A. Describe your dream as if you have already manifested it: I have… I am… I make…

Example; I am a dancer in a big Broadway show. I have a farm with lots of animals. I make the best cookies in the world.

B. Importance: This is how important your dream is to you. One is the lowest importance, and ten is the highest.

C. Dream Intention: The deeper emotional reasons for **why** you want your dream. Make a strong emotional connection.

With just a few words, bring yourself back to the emotional connection in your intention. Write one or a few different dream intentions.

Example: I desire to help cats that are in pain.

D. Benefits you think you and the world will receive from your dream. See the benefits of how your dream will change the life for yourself and others. Your mind needs to see a clear benefit or reward to move you in the right direction.

Example: All the animals in my village will get help. People will respect animals more.

E. Think of the **actions between where you are now and where you would like to be**. What actions are you taking to reach your dream? Be creative and think outside the box. Write as many as you like and think about the different ways to get to your dream. You need to see every step on your path to your dream, imagine what will happen, although it might be entirely different in the end. Then your mind will be able to create it into reality. Go back later and review what you have written, since the steps will change over time. Write each step as if you are already doing it.

Example: I am studying about cats. I am writing about it on the note board in the school or at work. I am informing people. I am holding a speech...

F. Give Thanks and write how grateful you are for already having achieved your dream. Be emotional. Try to feel how fantastic it feels having reached your dream and how thankful you are for having it.

Example: I feel inspired, motivated and joyous after taking action in helping the cats.

G. How will you celebrate yourself? What will you do to acknowledge your progress or each little step you take on your way to your dream? Define your rewarding system, which could be giving yourself a sweet, buying something, sharing the progress with your friends, having a party.

Example: For every cat I help, I will take or draw a picture of it and put it up on the wall to remind me that I am living my dream.

Conclusion

In the beginning, only focus on your dreams with an importance rating of 10. The highest rated dream is where you have the most passion and are more likely to manifest faster. Everything below the rating ten is not considered at this time. Hold the intention of your dream and remember: when you can clearly see and feel your dream, the outcome is already in creation. It's real although not visible; it's on its way to you.

Go back at least once a week and review your dream to change what doesn't feel right anymore. Remember, this is the plan of **your life** and the plan to manifest your dream. It will evolve over time, and this is fine. Just play, have fun and know it will happen.

Exercise Tool 2: **See Your Dream Already Manifested.**

Visualization: Sit down, take some deep breaths, relax and close your eyes.

Take time and visualize your dream, as you wrote it in your manifestation plan.

- Imagine your dream as if it's already happening.
- Feel how effortless it was to manifest it.
- Look back at each step you took to reach your dream.
- Feel the joy of having accomplished your goal.
- Feel how grateful you are for having achieved what you desire.
- See yourself celebrating your accomplishment.

STEP 5 | MANIFESTATION PLAN - YOUR DREAM PLAN

Exploring obstacles to your dream, and what to do if they hit you.

Confusion from too many options: If you have too many options of what you can do in your life, you have to make a choice. It could be choosing between what kind of education you want, or what kind of work you are going to do.

Maybe you have a different dream of how you want to live your life. When there are too many choices, it can create a significant internal stress. You don't know if you chose the right dream, so you start to ask your friends about it. They all have different ideas and dreams, which just adds to your confusion and stress.

You start to get frustrated because you can't get an answer for your questions from anyone outside of you. Internally, you are battling all your ideas and you finally get very confused.

When two or more ideas are struggling inside you, it ends up in confusion. If you continue dwelling over the choices, your mind will get foggy, overloaded with information and finally shut down and go blank. The mind has worked on overload with trying to give you an answer, looking at all angles and finally, it gets totally confused, so you don't have access to any information at all.

If this is happening to you:

- Stop asking for advice or listening to other people's opinions.
- Relax your mind, not dwelling upon the options.
- Move your body by doing exercise or nature walks.
- Focus on the thing that makes you totally happy in life, what you did in Step 3.
- Let the inspiration of what you love to do fill you; stay in that feeling until you get clear again.

When the Fears Appear.

We all have fears, and so do you. It is perfectly fine. Instinctual fears are a natural protection mechanism that serve you in any dangerous situation. They are there to keep you safe. If you see a snake or some other dangerous animal, you react out of fear to keep away. Most of us have lost touch with our instinctual fears and developed more imaginary fears.

STEP 5 | MANIFESTATION PLAN - YOUR DREAM PLAN

You can have fears of standing out, being different or being bullied or just not fitting in. You might also have fears from memories in the past and fears about the future because you can't control it. The fears go on and on in your mind and it can paralyze and completely control you. When the fear connects with a feeling, you start to believe it is real. This can turn into a vicious circle with no end.

Your mind only knows the past and will always fear the future, since it can't control it or understand it. It will start to discourage you, so that your dream will never happen. It can even threaten you that something negative will happen if you stay with your dream. It is a never-ending story - your mind will give you hundreds of reasons for why you can't do it, and some will be very convincing.

The way out is to stop struggling with your mind. Just observe it.

Watch your thoughts and listen to all the frightening things it tells you. Listen to the mind in the way you would listen to a frightened child. You know the little child just needs to be held, loved and told that it will be ok. This will calm the mind. Listen to it, observe it, and say it's ok to be scared. Then continue with your dream.

Fear of losing a job, by Mats Löfkvist

"I was newly married to my first wife and living in Vienna, Austria. As a foreigner, I was applying for hundreds of different jobs, which were all declined. Finally, I got a front desk position in a five-star hotel. I was the only male, and after a few months, the front office manager decided that I was too slow with computers, and fired me.

This was like a punch in the stomach, and I didn't know how we would survive financially. However, I knew that I had a passion for the hotel business. On my last day at work, I made a decision; to be a general manager for a big hotel in Vienna in five years' time.

After going through several different job positions in various hotels, I finally received an offer to be the General Manager for a new Swedish business hotel just three years after being fired from the first job. I refused to let the fear of rejection and the embarrassment of getting fired stop me from becoming what I knew I would become."

If this is happening to you:

- Don't fight the fears because they will win, and you will just lose your energy.
- Go back into the second step in the manual, sit and observe your thoughts and feelings connected to the fears.
- Through watching the fears, and knowing that they are only fears with no real connection to reality, you are not giving them energy and the fears will disappear. Focus instead on what makes you happy and what gives you inspiration.
- You'll probably need to keep observing your fears many times, since your mind always will create new fears.

STEP 5 | MANIFESTATION PLAN - YOUR DREAM PLAN

You forgot your dream.

It happens to all of us. As much as you dearly want your dream, daily life takes over, and suddenly you have forgotten that you had a dream. Then you get angry and frustrated with yourself, both from forgetting and from not following your internal inspiration of what makes you happy. Forgetting is natural and happens to everyone.

To remind you and prevent forgetting we ask you to write down every detail in your **Brave Dreaming Journal** and also using the **Manifestation Plan**. The plan will bring you right back into your dream. Go back and update your plan to make sure it is in line with what you desire and how you think it will happen.

*"I picked up my old journal written some thirty years ago. It was soothing to read that many of my dreams back then I have now accomplished. I also realized that my intention thirty years ago was the same as I have today. This made me understand that our deeper purpose stays with us for our whole life; it is just expressed in different ways during our lifetime". **-Maria Löfkvist***

It is great to keep track of ourselves to know that we, in fact, do what we want to do in life. Don't let go of your dream. Once you have been distracted from your dream for a while, make sure you go back and read your journal and remember your intention in the manifestation plan to get back on track again.

If this is happening to you:

Read the details in your Manifestation Plan and Brave Dreaming Journal.

- Go back into your "Dream Lab" and make your dream real again.
- Look at your manifestation plan and change it when you need to.
- Write notes everywhere in your home with "Remember to Dream."
- Write "Remember to Dream" notes in your calendar to remind yourself.
- Before sleeping, visualize yourself having and living your dream.

STEP 5 | MANIFESTATION PLAN - YOUR DREAM PLAN

 Summary:

- You made your manifestation plan and visualized it happening.
- You explored three different obstacles; confusion, fear and forgetting your dream.
- You gained tools: how to get past the obstacles.

 Summary Exercise Tools:

1. The manifestation plan
2. See your dream already manifested

 What you have done so far:

Step 1: You have made your dream lab.
Step 2: You are becoming aware of your thoughts and feelings.
Step 3: You are defining your dream with unlimited time and money.
Step 4: You are finding your intention and what you believe or know about your dream.
Step 5: You made your manifestation plan to make your dream real faster.

STEP 6
SENDING OUT YOUR DREAM

SENDING OUT YOUR DREAM

You know what you want and you can see your dream clearly in front of you.
You have checked your thoughts and feelings connected to your dream.
You know deep inside that your dream will happen.
You are ready to **take action**, sending it out.

Now is the time to be creative by finding ways outside the normal to communicate and express your dream to the world. Sending out your dream is something you will constantly do until your dream starts to come back to you.

What you do continuously becomes your everyday habit!

It would be great to think that you can lie on the couch watching television and eating popcorn, and your dream will come and knock on the door. Well, in a way, it will, but first you have to make sure you have sent it out regularly in one form or another.

It is like playing a team sport with yourself.

Let's imagine that you are on a football team. Start to warm up your muscles before the game. You need to know what position you have on the team. Once the team has practiced together for a while, it starts to flow more easily, and you get into a momentum that makes the whole game look easy, like it is happening on its own.

- **To warm up your muscles:**
  You are warming up your creativity and sending out your dream.

- **Knowing what sport you play and the position you have on the team:**
  Is to know your dream, your direction.

- **The team playing together in a natural flow:**
  Is when you start to hear back from people and your dream starts to get back to you, it goes back and forth.

- **The effortless-looking momentum in the game:**
  Is when the smooth flow happens. When the whole energy is flowing in the same direction; then your dream will be moving on its own.

As you can imagine, there are many players on the field to make a football game work, and it is the same idea in creating your dream. The fundamental thing is that **you** are the primary player, but also part of the whole team. You are essential to the game. You need to learn when to run and when to rest, so you don't deplete all of your energy at once. If you do, you don't have the strength to run again when the ball comes to you.

Life in general is much like this football game. We all need to learn when to take action and when to wait for the ball to come back to us. The essential part is to realize that you are the leading player of the game of your life, whichever position you have. Your dream game cannot happen without your active participation.

Now let's look at how you can make a habit of sending out your dream.

STEP 6 | SENDING OUT YOUR DREAM

How to Send Out Your Dream.

A: Through talking to people. Your dream will be sent out quickly through talking to people. Almost all connections that take place in life happen because of other people. Remember, you are not alone on the football field - you can't do your dream alone. You need support and information, which will come through talking to people.

As a young person, you need to talk to adults. They are the carrier of information and most of the time, the connection to other adults: they can help take you in the direction of your dream. That is one of the fastest ways of getting your dream out. Adults are also the carrier of life experiences.

Adults don't have the young creative mind that you have, so don't let anyone discourage you. Listen to their valuable information of how things work, how systems are set up, of how to approach another adult with whom you need to connect. Doing this protects you from making mistakes that other people have already made. It can save you months or years, so listen carefully to what they say. Then you make up your mind of what you want to do and how you want to do it.

You may feel shy when approaching and talking to adults, as they can be an authority figure. Just remember that they were also once kids and wore diapers. Now they are just big kids without diapers. Then you don't have to feel inferior, just treat them with respect.

Start to talk to the adults you have around you. Ask them if they have connections to take you in the direction of your dream. Then take action on the information and do it step by step.

B: Through writing articles, e-mails, or putting up notes or posting on the Internet. In addition to talking to people directly, there are many other ways to communicate.

<u>Without Using the Internet:</u>

1. Writing personal letters: Today it is very rare to receive a mailed, personal handwritten letter, and because of that, most people will open them and read them. Find out the address to the correct person and send them your letter.
2. Draw posters or write signs and put them up on local billboards.
3. Make handwritten fliers that you can share with people.

4. Write an article and send it to the newspapers and magazines. Writing it from a young mind's view of life, telling about your dream.
5. Try to find the places where you can write about or tell your dream to inspire others.
6. Call television stations to come and do a report on you or your dream work.
7. Hold speeches for students, adults or organizations doing similar things to your dream.
8. Make a play with your dream message and present it to others.
9. Ask for help, and invite other people join you.
10. Be a creative Brave Dreamer

<u>Using the Internet.</u>

1. Use social media like Facebook, Twitter, YouTube, Instagram, etc. to send out your message and inspire others.
2. Make your blog writing about your dream.
3. Make your website and keep it alive and updated.
4. Make your video on the steps to your dream and post it on YouTube.
5. Make personal contacts online to talk to people about your dream.

C: Through telling like-minded people who have already done it. It can be a friend, an older sibling, or an adult. Someone that has recently done what you want to do. These people usually love to share how they did it and they also know what problems you need to consider. They might have the contacts you need, and they probably know the next step you must take.

Talking to them also inspires you to know that it is possible to get to your dream and that there is a path to follow. If they could do it, so can you. These people are the most inspiring people to be around since they hold the same vision as you do.

D: Through forming groups. Create a group of friends who are all wanting something similar and work together. Start your Internet group or join in-person groups who share the same interests to inspire you.

Defining your Dream Statement.

Let's explore and elaborate on your dream statement by creating a short, concise, and compelling quote. You made your first dream statement in Step 3. Now it's time to refine it for easy, quick, and clear communication.

STEP 6 | SENDING OUT YOUR DREAM

Your newly elaborated dream statement will quickly communicate your vision to other people in a clear, precise way. We call this the "Elevator Speech," as it needs to be short enough to be said to someone else in an elevator before the ride is over.

In the business world, this is called the "USP," which stands for "Unique Selling Proposition," and it's known to be hugely important.

One of the most well-known and efficient USP's ever created, is the one Domino's Pizza used many years ago, which was "Fresh hot pizza delivered to your door in 30 minutes or less, or it's free." The statement was crystal clear and it changed Domino's from a small business to a huge company.

Source: Domino's Pizza Wikipedia.

Our USP is:

> ***Global Mentor Aid is a nonprofit, online mentoring program, inspiring young people worldwide to become future leaders.***

It tells you exactly:

What we do,
What kind of business we have,
Where we work, and,
What is our intention.

The USP is not set in stone and might change over time.

Exercise Tool 1: **Defining your dream statement.**

- Start with writing a longer statement that emotionally and logically make sense to you.
- Shorten it down to the very essence of your dream. Usually, you have to rewrite it many times before it sounds right.
- Make sure you include the intention of how it benefits you or the people involved.

My new dream statement is:

_____

_____

 Write it into your **Brave Dreaming Journal.**

How to Tell Your Dream.

1. Start by telling your new dream statement to as many people or in as many places as possible.
2. When you feel that someone gets interested in wanting to know more about your dream, you tell them your longer dream story.

Only tell your full dream story to the people that support you.

It is essential, as not everyone will understand your dream and want to help you.

STEP 6 | SENDING OUT YOUR DREAM

Practice telling your dream story with conviction and emotion.

- Tell your dream story without personal back thoughts about getting something in return.
- Tell your story with inspiration, as you can help others to reach their goal.
- Be their inspiration.
- Tell your story like you already have it now.
- Tell it everywhere it fits in: I dream of… I am on my way to my dream…
- Tell it with no attachment to how and when it will happen.

Exercise Tool 3: Send out your dream bubble visualization.

 Visualize:

- Close your eyes, take some deep breaths and relax your whole body.
- Visualize that you print your dream statement on a big red heart.
- Take the heart and put it into a big soap bubble.
- Put all your good intentions of WHY you desire your dream, inside the bubble.
- With your mind relaxed, send out the bubble with the heart inside, and see it gliding up into the sky where it goes exactly where it needs to go, without you controlling it.
- Let it disappear and trust that it will find its way to each person that will benefit from it.
- Trust that it will find its way to each situation that you need for your dream to come true.
- Let it go without attachment to where it goes.
- Let it go without attachment to how it will happen.
- Release it, trust and surrender.

Send out your dream bubble in the morning and before you go to bed. Send it out over and over as many times as you like.

STEP 6 | SENDING OUT YOUR DREAM

 Summary:

- You learned how to send out your dream and how to make your new dream statement.
- You did the visualization sending out your dream bubble.

 Summary Exercise Tools:

1. Defining your dream statement.
2. Send out your dream bubble visualization.

 What you have done so far:

Step 1: You have made your dream lab.
Step 2: You are becoming aware of your thoughts and feelings.
Step 3: You are defining your dream with unlimited time and money.
Step 4: You are finding your intention and what you believe or know about your dream.
Step 5: You made your manifestation plan to make your dream real faster.
Step 6: You are defining how you can send out your dream using your new dream statement.

STEP 7

RESEARCH ABOUT YOUR DREAM

RESEARCH ABOUT YOUR DREAM

To create your dream is to take one step at a time, always maintaining focus. You have started the repeated activity to send out your dream. There will always be a gap between sending it out and until it starts coming back to you. How long this time will be is never defined, and you can't push it. Depending on your dream, it can take anywhere between one day to one week or even months for it to come back.

This is not a passive waiting time. It is a valuable time that you can use to do more research about your dream. With more knowledge about what you want, you will see your whole dream more clearly. You might find you still have many questions, which weren't taken into consideration when you started your dream. Finding the answers keeps you motivated to continue dreaming. Doing your research will allow your mind to focus on what you desire continuously.

Research and find out as much as you can about your dream.

My Dream, by Maria Löfkvist

"Once I dreamt about traveling the whole world. My primary interest was the different world religions, and how they affected the personal dreams that people had. I also wanted to find out if there was a collective dream that everyone had, independent of their country, religion, social, and political situation.

STEP 7 | RESEARCH ABOUT YOUR DREAM

I knew what I wanted and I could see it in front of me, but I lacked information. I needed to read up on all the religions to understand the different beliefs. I also needed to learn facts about the countries. How to get there, where to go, what to see, how to get in contact with the people, where I could find my answers.

I needed to know the weather conditions, when to travel to certain areas, what visa I needed, how much the hostels would cost, and how much money I needed every day. I had to spend a long time preparing myself before I could make the trip. During my preparation, I studied and worked part-time. When I had my information, I had finished school and saved the money to travel.

I made my dream come true and was able to travel through a dozen countries, meeting with beautiful people and having deep conversations about life.

I found that our collective dream is first to have our basic needs meet, and later to develop our inner potential, expressing it into the world."

Take an active part, but don't push.

Manifesting your dream is not about sitting around, waiting for it to happen. You need to be as active as possible to move energy in the direction of your dream. Take an active part, but don't push. We know that sounds contradictory, but if you come from a place of inspiration when you do your research, then there is no need to push, and it is not hard.

Remember, this is not work; it's about following your dream, which will make you happy, inspired and full of energy. It must be easy and fun to find out all the information you need.

The research will fill you with energy so that you can't wait to continue. You need to feel hungry for the information; just wanting to know more all the time.

It is not work.

If you see your dream as work, you are probably pushing yourself too hard. That will take away the inspiration and leave you with your mind pressing and pushing for results. Meanwhile, you lose your creativity and get frustrated because the dream is not happening fast enough. You might also find out that deep down, you didn't have enough interest to follow through to realize your dream. Maybe you figured out that it wasn't your real dream to start with, that you made it up to make somebody else happy, like your family, a loved one, friends or teachers.

Make sure it is your own dream.

Sometimes you believe you want a certain dream, but it is first when you become crystal clear about your dream, that you may realize if you want it or not. Your dream might seem more fun and easy when other people are doing it, and you think you also want the same dream. As long as you have limited information and your dream stays fuzzy, everything looks easy and fun. As you discover the activities and energy you need to spend in bringing it into reality, the fun might fade away.

If you have lost your inspiration and motivation to bring this dream into reality, it is entirely okay. The sooner you find out your real feelings, the better. If you feel you don't want to continue, you just start over again, going into the dream lab to make another dream that is yours. Deep down inside yourself you have one, believe me.

STEP 7 | RESEARCH ABOUT YOUR DREAM

Where can I start to research about my dream?

- Go to the library and look for books and magazines with articles about your dream. Read up on what others have already done. You don't have to invent the wheel, use the information and experiences from other people or groups.

- Find related images, videos and other content related to your dream. Use the library or YouTube and watch old movies related to your idea. Pay attention to how they solved their problems in the past. Take the old knowledge and combine it with new insights. In between the two, search for new inventions.

- Find out if you need any additional information or education. Are there any courses or lectures in your community that you can attend? Be creative to locate the training you need. If you want a special education, read up on it. Make sure you know everything about it to make it as real as possible.
  Example: *What does it mean to become a doctor? Where are they working? What do they do? What hours do they work? What specialties are there?*

- Are there any legal or economic perspectives to your dream? Do you need to open a company? Break down your dream into parts, and look for what information you need that is relevant for your dream to become real.

- Do you need permits, licenses, insurance or other papers? Don't hesitate to call government agencies or legal consultants for information; that's why they are there, to answer your questions. There are always organizations that will help you for free, even just to point you in the right direction.

Exercise Tool 1: Brainstorm how to research your dream.

Answer to the questions below:

- At which location will you start your dream?
- What can you do to research about it?
- What additional knowledge do you need?
- With whom do you need to make contact?
- Where, in addition to what you already have done, can you send out or share your dream?

STEP 7 | RESEARCH ABOUT YOUR DREAM

- Are there any local events, places, situations where you can take part?
- Are there any people in your area doing the same thing that you want to do?
- Can you visit these places to get the real feel of it?

 Write it down in your **Brave Dreaming Journal**.

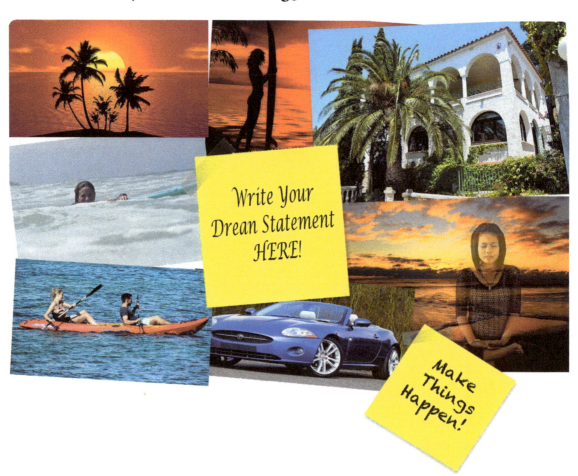

Exercise Tool 2: **Make a dream board.**

A dream board is a creative and fun way to remind yourself of your dream.

- Use any board, a piece of paper or cardboard.
- Start with writing your Dream Statement in the middle of the paper, and circle it with colors as the primary focus.
- Cut out from magazines, newspapers or self-drawn pictures, anything that represents your dream and glue them to the board.
- Make quotes that inspire you to remember your dream.
- Fill the whole paper with your dream.
- Look at your dream board every morning and at night, to remind yourself that your dream is on its way to you, now.

For online "Dream Board" creation, search for:

- Vision Board Apps for mobile phones
- Online "*Dream Board*" Makers
- Create one to use as your desktop image.

 Summary:

- You brainstormed how and where you can research about your dream, while you are waiting for it to come back to you.
- You made a dream board to remind yourself that your dream is on its way.

STEP 7 | RESEARCH ABOUT YOUR DREAM

 Summary Exercise Tools:

1. Brainstorm how to research your dream.
2. Make a dream board.

 What you have done so far:

Step 1: You have made your dream lab.
Step 2: You are becoming aware of your thoughts and feelings.
Step 3: You are defining your dream with unlimited time and money.
Step 4: You are finding your intention and what you believe or know about your dream.
Step 5: You made your manifestation plan to make your dream real faster.
Step 6: You are defining how you can send out your dream using your new dream statement.
Step 7: You are brainstorming where and how you can research about your dream.

STEP 8

LOOK FOR THE SIGNS

Look for the Signs

Start to look for the dream signs as they come back to you.

What signs? You send out your dream with a strong intention (the why) that serves as a magnet. It will start to come back to you through signs. Signs are like hidden messages that only you will see, feel and sense. You have to play detective to begin finding and understanding them. With practice, you will become an expert.

It is gratifying to be able to train yourself to recognize, see and feel the signs. Especially since they will take you to the next step towards your dream. Signs can come in various shapes and forms. You have to keep yourself open, receptive and curious to be able to see and sense them.

Even though you never know how the signs will show up, there are usually three ingredients to the recipe.

Inspiration, Intuition, and Synchronicity.

Inspiration

A sign that will enhance your inspiration of your dream. It will come with a feeling of, "Yeah, this feels fun, good and right." It feels light and joyous and you want more of it.

Always do what you feel inspired to do first. Say you have a list of tasks to do, like working, studying, cooking, washing clothes, cleaning your room, exercising and working on your dream. You know you need to do it all, but maybe you can choose in what order to do them.

Always start with what you feel most inspired to do. Maybe you think you'll never get around to do the dull cleaning, but you do. Somehow, when you allow yourself to follow your inspiration, you get everything done and it is effortless and fun.

Start to pay daily attention to where your inspiration lies. Then become aware of what makes you inspired in relation to your dream, which is usually a sign from your dream coming back to you.

What signs can look like:

- You see someone on the street that reminds you of somebody else that you need to contact.
- You have recurrent thoughts in your head that you need to go somewhere, look at something, or talk to somebody.
- You read a billboard, see a movie or commercial that gives you the answer to the next step towards your dream.
- Someone unexpected shows up talking about similar dream content, giving you the answer to your questions.
- If you see the same person showing up in various places, it's good to talk to that person.
- You read about a matter in a book that reminds you of your dream.
- You have a sleeping dream that gives you a message of what to do.
- You have a memory from the past that reminds you of your dream.
- Listen well to **all** conversations for information regarding your dream.

STEP 8 | LOOK FOR THE SIGNS

When you have a powerful feeling of inspiration to act, it is usually a sign.

"When the student is ready, the teacher will appear."
Buddha

Clear Signs, by Mats Löfkvist

"Recently, my mother reminded me that ever since I was a young child, I had been talking about living on an island in the South Pacific. I had long ago forgotten all about it. Decades later when I was traveling the world, I arrived at the South Pacific island of Samoa. As I stepped out of the plane, feeling the warm, humid air filled with the fragrance of the tropics, I just knew this was my home. I knew nothing about the island, but my heart felt at peace and happy.

I was playing tourist on the island and jokingly I kept asking myself; where is my family? Four days before I left the island, I was introduced to a young, beautiful Samoan lady. I instantly knew in my heart that it had happened; I had found my wife, my origin and my soul family. I finally had come home."

Intuition

"When the student is ready the teacher will appear" is a useful explanation for signs. Signs don't always come as you expect them to, or when you want them to. As you are the student in the saying above, you have to make yourself ready for the teacher to appear. The way to prepare yourself is to learn to listen within yourself. Listen to your intuition. The more you can come into contact with your internal voice of what feels right, the more you will see the signs. That is how you receive the teacher.

Your intuition is your inner guide. Your intuition will direct you, showing what is right or wrong for you. It serves as your inner compass to keep you on track. Your intuition speaks in countless ways. A hunch in your stomach, a new idea, a feeling of something being right, easy, light and joyous. It gives you a sense of expansion and flow and an internal knowing that you are moving in the right direction. When you feel a constriction or pain in your stomach that is thick and hard, then your intuition is telling you that something is not good for you.

Remember to be careful about mistaking this easy feeling with the actions you will be taking – just because the feeling came easy does not mean that what you have to do is easy. Your intuition will point you in the direction of where you need to take action. If you follow your inner guide, you will reach your goal faster.

STEP 8 | LOOK FOR THE SIGNS

These are a few of the subtle ways that your intuition speaks:

- You feel like bringing an umbrella even if the sun is shining.
- You feel the urge to go someplace, but you don't know why.
- You feel you need to call someone without knowing why.
- An idea continues to jump up in your head.

Program your mind to look for signs everywhere, then you will start to see them faster.

Synchronicity

You are a piece of a much bigger puzzle, called life. It is a puzzle with no visible end. It moves in its own way and most of the time we don't understand how and why.

Imagine your life's possibilities as countless colored pieces of your life puzzle, floating around above you in space. Since there is an abundance of pieces, you don't know exactly how and when they will fall down to create your life. When a piece falls (a sign), you need to be prepared to see how it will fit in by doing the following:

- Feeling the flow of your inspiration.
- Using your intuition to have an internal knowing of whether it's right or wrong for you.
- Using the synchronicity as a guide to tell you if you are on your path or not.

Synchronicity reveals itself in the events that are happening to you, events that you in no way could create yourself:

- You meet a friend that you haven't met in many years.
- You get money unexpectedly, just at the time you needed it.
- You were delayed getting to work, only to learn that this saved you from being in an accident.

Events made by synchronicity are situations you can't foresee, have a say in, or control. They are part of your big life-puzzle, and it is up to you to find out how they fit into your life.

Life is a Paradox. A paradox means that at least two or more conditions are happening at the same time with a contradictory nature. The paradox here is that as much as you try to create your dream, you are not in control of the outcome. You are not always responsible or having a say in all that happens to you in your life. There are situations that you can't control and that you also didn't create.

STEP 8 | LOOK FOR THE SIGNS

Knowing this takes off the massive burden of guilty feelings that may result when you think you are responsible if a tragedy happens to you. When you have the choice to act, use your intuition on what actions to take. If you can do something about your situation, good. **If not, let it go. Go with the flow and accept what is.**

Not everything is a sign. Not everything you see will be a sign for you. If you start to see too many signs everywhere, you can't follow up on all of them. To get clarity, use your intuition, "Does it feel right and expansive inside?"

Signs DO NOT feel like this:

- Signs do not force you.
- They do not create great urgency.
- They are not needy or greedy.
- They never contain guilt or blame.

If you have these feelings provoked inside of you, know that it's not a sign.

Sometimes we so desperately want something to be a sign that our feelings run wild and the mind makes it up, especially if you are looking for love. You may take a beautiful smile as a sign, when in reality, the person smiles to everybody. Use your intuition to differentiate. Take a deep breath and pay attention to how the sign feels inside. If you feel confused not knowing what to do, then do like the masters:

"If you don't know what to do - don't do anything. Sleep on it."

Taking a break is a good way to cool your emotions. Sleeping on it for at least one night also helps. The next day, check for your inspiration and intuition. Then you will know if it was a sign or not.

 Exercise Tool 1: The Signs of the Day

Sit down, relax and take some deep breaths.

Start to go through in your mind all that happened during the day.

STEP 8 | LOOK FOR THE SIGNS

Start with you waking up and continue on through your day looking for signs. Don't just look at your daily routines; look for signs in conversations, actions, people you met, inspirations you had, thoughts or ideas you remember.

 Bring forward every possible sign about your dream and write it all down in your **Brave Dreaming Journal**.

 Write down in your Brave Dreaming Journal the answers to these questions:

- What gave me inspiration today?
- What did I intuit today about my dream?
- What synchronicities happened today?
- Sleep on it. If you have the same inspiration the following day, follow up on it.

 Summary:

- You recognize what signs are and what they can look like.
- You learned about your inspiration, intuition, and synchronicity.
- You know what signs don't feel like.

Summary Exercise Tools:

1. The signs of the day.

What you have done so far:

Step 1: You have made your dream lab.
Step 2: You are becoming aware of your thoughts and feelings.
Step 3: You are defining your dream with unlimited time and money.
Step 4: You are finding your intention and what you believe or know about your dream.
Step 5: You made your manifestation plan to make your dream real faster.
Step 6: You are defining how you can send out your dream using your new dream statement.
Step 7: You are brainstorming where and how you can research about your dream.
Step 8: You are recognizing signs through using your inspiration, intuition, and synchronicity.

STEP 9

TAKING ACTION ON THE SIGNS

Taking Action on the Signs

Now it is finally time to take action on the signs. Up until now, you've done lots of homework and worked on yourself. Now you are ready to start to express your dream into the world.

You are clear on what you want, you have defined it and made it into a statement. You don't just believe it, you know you can have it. You have done your research about it. You sent it out in various ways. You see and sense the signs coming back to you.

You are ready to take action!

Scared to Take Action?

To take action can feel scary. You might think that you don't yet have enough information about your dream. You could still be waiting to get more education, or you don't know if you have done enough research. It might feel scary to approach the person you know you need to contact. It feels safe and secure where you are, and unsafe outside in the unknown.

It is perfectly normal to feel this way. You have been doing all this preparation and now suddenly you need to reach out and make your dream real. It is time to deeply connect with your inner inspiration to make it stronger than your fear. Now you need to be the ***Brave Dreamer.***

> ***"Don't wait; the right time will never come."***
> *- Napoleon Hill*

Don't wait for the perfect situation, the perfect time, or for yourself to become perfect. It won't happen. None of us are perfect, so don't put that pressure on yourself. There will always be more you can do and learn to prepare yourself, but for right now it is enough, so don't let that stop you. **You are ready to take action, NOW.**

Which action should I take?

Which action you take depends on what signs have come back to you. Remember that you need to go from your inside and out, meaning you use your inner resources – your inspiration and intuition - to know which action to take.

STEP 9 | TAKING ACTION ON THE SIGNS

The Important thing is to take that first step. Bravely overcoming one small fear gives you the courage to take on the next...
- Daisku Ikeda

If you have many signs and you don't know which one to act on first, follow your inspiration. Sit with the feeling of each sign and feel the level of inspiration it gives you. Whichever sign is most **connected to your heart** and not the head, this is the sign you need to act on.

Choose, How to Take Action!

Use your mind to brainstorm; how can you take action on your signs of inspiration?

For example: If you felt a strong need to talk to a person. Then think about what would be the best way to approach this person.

Maybe talking directly, or making an appointment, perhaps writing a letter or calling on the phone. Let your mind become creative to choose what seems right at the moment, then don't think too much, take action, **just do it**.

- Make that appointment with the person.
- Make that call.
- Go to that meeting.
- Write that letter.
- Just talk directly spontaneously.
- Follow your inspiration. Just do it!

Exercise Tool 1: **Get Clear on Which Action to Take.**

Visualize:

- Sit and take some deep breaths and relax.
- Start to go through in your mind all that happened during the day.
- Do the "*Signs of the day*" exercise in Step 8.
- Make a list of all the signs that have come back to you.
- Pay attention to your inspiration level with each of the signs.
- Write down how you will take action on the signs. Start with the one that gives you the strongest feeling of inspiration.
- Sleep on it. If you have the same inspiration the following day, make sure you follow up on it.
- Update your **Manifestation Plan** (Step 5) with your new action plan.

STEP 9 | TAKING ACTION ON THE SIGNS

 Write it down in your **Brave Dreaming Journal.**

"Our greatest glory is not in never falling but in rising every time we fall."
Confucius

*Will you fail?
NO, but you might fall.*

You can never fail; you can only learn. There isn't anything called failing, but you can fall. If you fall, you get up, analyze the situation and learn from it. Both falling and succeeding are blessings. Sometimes falling is a better teacher than succeeding, so never see falling as something negative; it's truly there to help you.

We all learned to walk when we were kids. When you fell, didn't you get up again and try to take another step? It's not a matter of how many times you fall, what matters is how many times you stand up again and continue your mission. You need to walk your dream with the same determination, and recognize that side steps or falls do not mean failure.

If you get an **"no,"** it is not a failure; it is help. It gives you an insight of what **not** to do. A no just indicates that this wasn't the right time, person or situation for you. It also shows that the **"right"** time, person, or circumstances for your dream is still yet to come.

Thomas Edison apparently fell 10,000 times before he succeeded in creating the light bulb. Yes! It is scary to take action, but you have to be brave and do it anyways.

"I have not failed. I've just found 10,000 ways that won't work."
Thomas Edison

Don't take things personally. When you allow your personal feelings of resistance, insecurity, and fear to come up, it will block you from taking the next step. When you feel resistance, it is easy to believe that it is all about you being or doing something wrong. Don't take anything personal; do the best you can and follow through to take action. If you fall, stand up again and continue. When you see good results from your actions, you will get out of your fear and realize that the problem wasn't about you.

Accept that you have fears and do it anyway. You **will have** resistance, fears, and insecurities. It is all normal. You **cannot** defeat or erase those fears. They will not go away, so it is a useless fight. You will just lose your energy and become more insecure, thinking you need to be fearless. Just accept that you have fears. Observe them and make friends with them. Don't analyze them too much. If you've done your homework, just take action. Be brave and do it.

 Exercise Tool 2: **If you can't get out of your fears.**

- Go back to Step 2 and work with the feelings to clarify the fear.
- Write down all your fears.
- Look at each fear like a small child that wants attention.
- Get to know each of them, hold them, embrace them and love them.
- Decide to take action.
- Tell each fear that you will take action anyway and that they have to support you.
- If they come up when you take action, recognize them; "Oh, this is my little fear of failure," hold it and love it, don't get scared of it.

STEP 9 | TAKING ACTION ON THE SIGNS

Trust in Yourself. We are telling you to have a big chunk of trust. Yes, have confidence in yourself. You have made a strong internal connection, now you are feeling your inspiration and trusting your intuition. Take action and use your intuition as a guide for what to do. You can be certain that when you take the first action step, the next step will come to you.

When you take one step forward, you won't stand on one leg forever. The next step will appear, but you have to take the first step and trust.

Summary:

- You learned how to take action on your dream.
- You know what to do when fears come up.
- You updated your "Manifestation Plan" with steps to take now.

 Summary Exercise Tools:

1. Get clear on which action to take.
2. What to do if you can't get out of your fears.

 What you have done so far:

Step 1: You have made your dream lab.
Step 2: You are becoming aware of your thoughts and feelings.
Step 3: You are defining your dream with unlimited time and money.
Step 4: You are finding your intention and what you believe or know about your dream.
Step 5: You made your manifestation plan to make your dream real faster.
Step 6: You are defining how you can send out your dream using your new dream statement.
Step 7: You are brainstorming where and how you can research about your dream.
Step 8: You are recognizing signs through using your inspiration, intuition, and synchronicity.
Step 9: You took action on your dream and you know you can't fail; only fall.

STEP 10
ACCEPTANCE

STEP 10 | ACCEPTANCE

ACCEPTANCE

We sincerely want to acknowledge you for being brave enough to follow through with each step in creating your dream. You are well on your way to building your future.

Remember, you are Unique. There is only **one** of you, and that is you. That is why you sometimes feel different than others, because you *are* special - the only one of your kind.

You are here to express this uniqueness that you have. Show people who you are and let others enjoy your special gift. When you live your dream, you show your personal gift and you share it with others. If anyone in your life told you that you are not unique, it was because they couldn't see who you truly are.

The problem might also be that **YOU** can't see yourself, who **YOU** really are. When you finally see and accept your uniqueness, then you will accept and love yourself as you are. Acceptance of other people, situations and circumstances starts with yourself. Only when you can fully accept and love yourself will you be able to accept and love others.

Finally, you will have more tolerance and love for everything and everybody around you. Of course, none of us are perfect and all of us do un-perfect things in life. You too, and it is ok.

Accepting and loving yourself is the road to accepting and loving others.

Acceptance does not mean holding on to people or situations that harm you or don't serve your purpose in life. Sometimes we choose to permit certain conditions around us, thinking that we are victims of the circumstances and that we can't change our choices.

You have the power to change **YOUR** choices, but not other people's choices. It is important to see with your inner eye, your feelings and intuition, what is going on behind the surface, and to make conscious choices in life.

Change the situation if you can, if not, accept it and let it go.

To accept what is. When you accept situations and people as they are, especially yourself as you are, you will allow for valuable life lessons to be learned, which can change the future for yourself and others. By accepting, you will enable life to work out its magic in a way that you will not always logically understand.

STEP 10 | ACCEPTANCE

Remember, you can't change the past and you can't control the future. In reality, you are not in control of anything at all above **your choice in the present moment.**

All you have is a choice in the present moment.

The present moment is now and now and now...

Not everything is meant to be changed. When you see an upcoming life situation heading in an unwanted direction, it can produce a high level of fear, tension, and frustration. The natural instinct is to take action to try and prevent it from happening.

Some examples of this could be:

- You tried your best but didn't get the grades to enter school or that perfect job.
- Not being able to pay back a bank loan.
- You realize that your partner will never change, independent of what you do.

When you have taken all possible steps to prevent an unwanted outcome and it's still happening, there are lessons to be learned. You have analyzed all possible angles of the situation, but you couldn't get a solution. In the end, it comes to a point when you need to **accept what is and surrender**, as you can't change it. It truly isn't meant to be changed.

Sometimes you have to allow your friends, family or partner to make mistakes, which will be crucial for their learning in life. Many people only learn from their mistakes, regardless of what you are telling them. Do not interfere with lessons that could be of great importance for their lives.

Incidences in life often appear to make you aware of other solutions or directions to your current situation. They will take you on the path where you need to go. To resist these incidents means to resist the progress that life offers you. In truth, whatever is presented to you, regardless of whether you consider it good or bad, always appears to help you to move forward. So, in the end, all is good.

Accept what is and give life a possibility to give you what is meant to be. It could be something entirely different from what you expected. These opportunities come to you once you let go of your attachment to changing the situation.

Yes! It will come on its own; you just have to be brave first to let go.

Acceptance and Synchronicity, by Mats Löfkvist

After ending my four-year naval academy study in Sweden, I decided to follow my dream of sailing around the world. In a newspaper ad, I found a group of people building a yacht and

STEP 10 | ACCEPTANCE

they were supposed to sail around the world. I became part of the team; it was perfect for me since I learned everything about boat building. However, it took more than a year to finish the yacht, twice the estimated time.

Shortly before Christmas in freezing cold weather, we sailed away from Sweden to Denmark, dreaming about the coming warm and beautiful climate, in a not too distant future. The winter got worse and the ice froze on the sea, making it impossible to continue. We were stuck for the rest of the winter. I felt disappointed, having a crushed dream, but I needed to accept the situation as it was. I decided to go back to Sweden, buy a ticket to any warm place, and just see what happens.

On the train back to Sweden, I spoke to a young girl who told me about a Swedish company that owned luxury charter yachts in the Caribbean. When I arrived, I immediately contacted the company. They were currently looking for crew members for their yachts. Only two weeks later, I was in the Caribbean, doing exactly what I had been dreaming of. This was the start of many years' work as a captain of different sailing yachts, crossing the Atlantic Ocean ten times.

Exercise Tool 1: **A test to determine whether to change or accept your situation.**

Think about a situation you want to change.

Consider every angle of the situation carefully before you try to change anything:

- Analyze the reason WHY you want to create a change.
- Analyze the worst thing that can happen if you accept the situation.

- Analyze the best thing that can happen if you accept the situation.
- Look for what you can learn from the present situation, if you don't change it.
- Do you recognize it as a recurrent situation in your life; has some similar situation happened before?
- Check if it **is possible** to change the situation you are in, or do you spend your energy resisting something that is not meant to be changed?

Look for the honest answers and use your intuition to decide whether to change or accept the situation. Write down your answers in your **Brave Dreaming Journal**.

Accept what is and be happy now. Don't wait for some special occasion, circumstance or conditional love to come for you to be happy. You are wasting your time, **be happy now.** If you are not happy now, you will not be happy when you have reached your dream. Real happiness comes from inside - not outside of you. Happiness is not a destination; it's something essential you need for your journey.

Have you ever told yourself…..

- I will be happy when I get that new job.
- I will be happy when I get a new home.
- I will be happy when I find my perfect love.
- I will be happy when I have more time.
- I will be happy when I have more money.

The truth is, everything external (outside of you) will only make you happy for a short time. As soon as you have it, there will be something new that you want. It is a never-ending cycle that can only be interrupted by finding lasting happiness from inside.

When you are happy with yourself on the inside, you lose your attachment to what you desire. You are happy regardless of whether you have it or not. When you have reached this state of acceptance and inner happiness, the creative force attempts to give you all that you desire.

Yes, it sounds backward, but that is how it works.

- Be genuinely happy now, with the job you have.
- Feel grateful and happy for the house you live in, at this moment.
- Look forward to a great loving partner, but be happy now with the present life you currently have.
- Just be authentically satisfied with the amount of money you have now and know that more is on its way.

The whole experience of loving yourself happens within you. Regardless of where you are, who you are, what you've done in your life and what you believe, *learning to love yourself is the greatest gift of all.*

You might be so busy that you don't take the time to stop and receive love. Maybe you run around in your rat race believing that love is something that has to come to you. Or that it's only possible to be expressed through some other person, who will show it to you. Maybe you learned that love is conditioned and needs to be expressed in a particular manner, otherwise it is not love.

Loving yourself is an internal state, and does not depend on external events or people. When you feel love and acceptance for yourself, you open up to receive the love energy that is all around you. You start to focus on love instead of fear.

Love is not some feeling that happens to you by chance. Yes, maybe to fall in love with someone can happen by chance. To feel love is an internal experience independent of outer circumstances. That's why learning to love yourself is the greatest gift of all.

The more you love yourself, the more love you will receive and give. You are your own personal gauge of how much love you will receive in life. Re-focus your attention from your mind down to your heart. Consciously open up your heart and your feelings and be willing to receive love. Open up to see love everywhere with your eyes, feel the love with your senses, smell, taste love in whatever you bring into your mouth. Hear love in the music and speak love with your words.

> *The more you love yourself, the faster you will manifest*
> *your dream, as you will feel worthy of receiving it.*

If not now, then when?

When in your life are you going to love yourself and receive love?

- Later, once you have become that perfect person that deserves it?
- Or when you have more money or better grades?
- Or when you have the material possessions that seem so important?
- Or when you worked out your hard childhood issues and released the pain?

- Or once you meet your perfect partner?
- Or when someone, at last, acknowledges the hard work that you have done?

Whatever your thoughts or feelings are, the fastest way to manifest your dream and be happy lies in your ability to; *"Love yourself and to accept what is."*

Start to practice NOW.

Yes! You do need to practice because you haven't received your dream yet. Take the opportunity to practice in this very instant and every chance you get.

- ***Now is the time*** to receive the happy events that your heart desires.
- ***Now is the time*** to accept yourself and open yourself up to receive love.
- ***Now is the time*** to accept what is.
- ***Now is the time*** to be happy!

Are you only reading this, or can you feel it inside?

If you only read it with your mind, it will just be more words.

Stop, take it into your heart, and feel it.

- Accept yourself, see how you are special.
- Love yourself as you are.
- Be happy and accept what is now.

STEP 10 | ACCEPTANCE

Remember that so far you have been successfully managing every single situation that has happened in your life, and you will manage every future situation as well. Have no fear, just accept what is.

- Let go of your fear and trust the future.
- Accept circumstances and people for what and who they are.
- Give thought to every situation and change it if you feel you can.
- If you can't change it, it's not meant to be changed.
- Let it go and accept what is.

Love yourself for who you are and be happy in whatever situation you have. Understand that life has given you this opportunity to evolve into something more and greater. It just might not look that way when you are in the middle of a situation.

Love yourself and know you are always going in the right direction. The question is, are you listening to what your heart and intuition tell you?

 Summary:

- You learned the importance of accepting yourself, as is.
- You learned that not everything is meant to be changed.
- You know that happiness and fulfillment come from inside.
- You understand that loving yourself is the greatest gift of all.

Summary Exercise Tool:

1. Test to see if you are changing or accepting your situation.

 What you have done so far:

Step 1: You have made your dream lab.
Step 2: You are becoming aware of your thoughts and feelings.
Step 3: You are defining your dream with unlimited time and money.
Step 4: You are finding your intention and what you believe or know about your dream.
Step 5: You made your manifestation plan to make your dream real faster.
Step 6: You are defining how you can send out your dream using your new dream statement.
Step 7: You are brainstorming where and how you can research about your dream.
Step 8: You are recognizing signs through using your inspiration, intuition, and synchronicity.
Step 9: You know when to take action on your dreams and that you can't fail, only fall.
Step 10: You are accepting what is in life, knowing that happiness and love are an inside job.

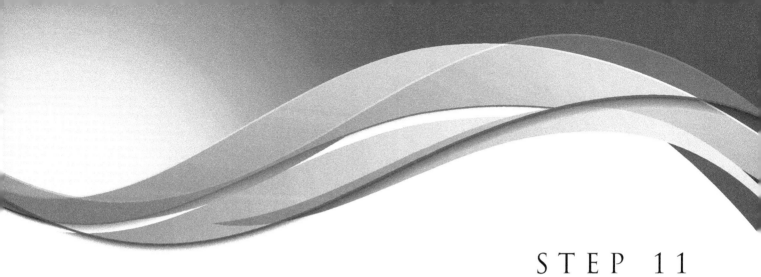

STEP 11
BE PATIENT AND TRUST

Be Patient and Trust

You Are Not Alone.

We like you to know that this is a real journey and the steps of creation are the same for everyone. You are not alone, and we know what you are facing.

As for us writing this book, we have personally gone through every creation step to get to this chapter. Just as you have, we are working on manifesting our dream, and YOU are our dream.

Our story:

"Mats and I (Maria) hadn't seen each other more than once every four years, and we hadn't been keeping in touch. Mats had been living in Samoa, an island in the South Pacific Ocean, and I had been residing in Mexico for the last twenty years. We met in Sweden at a family reunion, walked together in the forest and found that we had a shared dream. We had been living very different lives than most people. The main ingredients for both of us were that we had been very brave. We also had separately done a lot of introspective research, with meditation and consciousness training.

"We both had an intense inner yearning to give over this knowledge to young people. We thought that if we had access to this information when we were young, a manual that took us step by step through the creation process, we would have made less mistakes throughout life. This inspiration started our dream intention, to share our experiences in the form of an online course and a book.

"Even though we knew what we wanted, it took a long time to become totally clear about the dream, which by the way is the hardest part. We had to go through all of our thoughts, feelings, and fears before we could define what we were doing and how to express it.

"To be brave doesn't mean you don't have fears. All of us have fears, and so do we. Especially when there was a long time gap when nothing happened, between sending out our dream and it starting to come back. We were working part-time jobs to make ends meet. We realized that the more we worked on our fears as they appeared, the faster the project started to flow.

"The interesting thing was when we started the project, we had no fear. As we continued, all sorts of unrealistic fears popped up, but we were always willing to go back to the second step to work out our thoughts and feelings. Step by step, we could release the fears and negative feelings and move forward.

"The fact that you are reading this book now makes our dream come true. The way that you utilize this knowledge shortens the time and difficulty for you to reach what you desire. It is not a smooth journey to reach your dream. But when you feel called to do something, it doesn't matter how hard it is or how long it takes, you just don't give up.

"We are reaching our dream when we are helping you in reaching yours. So, don't give up on yourself, your dream or thinking that something is impossible. Only you can create your life and your dream. Don't wait for anyone else to do it for you, because you will end up standing still waiting.

"You have to ride the waves as they come, just as we have done. You must trust in yourself and your dream, knowing that it is all possible. Remember, you never fail, only fall. Then you stand up again, analyze and continue."

Trust in Your Process.

At this point in your process, relax and release any tension from trying to direct and control your dream. Just let go and trust.

Yes, we know it sounds contradictory, but that's how it is.

- First, you have to make your dream entirely clear with all the steps.
- Then you need to put it on a backburner and just hold on to the intention, without forcing it.
- Trust that as long as you hold a clear dream vision, your dream intention, the energy you sent out **will** come back to you at the perfect time and in a perfect way.
- Trust that you have the ability to recognize your dream when it comes.
- Have faith in the perfection of how it will unfold.

Sounds like a lot of trusts, and that is why you have to be brave.
You have to give it over to life, with no attachment to the outcome.

Be Patient and Trust. Patience and trust are two big words. They sometimes seem impossible, and you can get overwhelmed or confused by the fact that you need to trust and let go.

You can look at it logically if you have done your homework sending out your dream. There are enormous amounts of energies working on sending it back to you. During this time in between, you have to wait patiently. It is like putting an ad in the newspaper; you don't know exactly the effect this will have, but you know that the energy is working in your direction. Now you need to wait for it to come back and let go of the attachment to knowing how it will come back. You can trust in that it will appear at the perfect time and in a perfect way.

STEP 11 | BE PATIENT AND TRUST

Be patient; remember to take every step as it comes and to trust that the next step will appear.

Trust that you can recognize your next step. The more you can relax into whatever happens, letting go of the outcome, the stronger you can hold and send out your dream intention.

When you are relaxed, you are more open-hearted and attentive to receive. Your mind becomes more flexible and your whole being is sensitive and responsive to anything that has to do with your dream.

When you are relaxed, you will recognize the next step to take. You will see the signs and know when to act. Trust that it will all come to you effortlessly, at the right time and in the right way.

 Summary:

- You learned to be patient and trust that your dream is on its way to you.
- By being relaxed, you know that you will recognize the next step to take.

 What you have done so far:

Step 1: You have made your dream lab.
Step 2: You are becoming aware of your thoughts and feelings.
Step 3: You are defining your dream with unlimited time and money.
Step 4: You are finding your intention and what you believe or know about your dream.
Step 5: You made your manifestation plan to make your dream real faster.
Step 6: You are defining how you can send out your dream using your new dream statement.
Step 7: You are brainstorming where and how you can research about your dream.
Step 8: You are recognizing signs through using your inspiration, intuition, and synchronicity.
Step 9: You know when to take action on your dreams and that you can't fail, only fall.
Step 10: You are accepting what is in life, knowing that happiness and love is an inside job.
Step 11: You are understanding the importance of trust, patience and the perfection of life.

STEP 12

CELEBRATE AND GIVE THANKS

STEP 12 | BE PATIENT AND TRUST

CELEBRATE AND GIVE THANKS

Celebrate who you are and who you have become. Most times we don't recognize ourselves for what we have done in our life. We take it for granted or simply forget it. For this reason, it's critical to write down what you accomplished and the knowledge you have already gained, then celebrate it.

Don't wait for your final dream to happen before you celebrate. Your life is made up of many small achievements over time. Every little success leads you into more clarity and brings you one step closer to your dream. Take the time to recognize them all and celebrate them.

When you forget to celebrate, you feel indifferent to what you accomplished, especially if this is over a long period of time. These long-time accomplishments could be finishing school, building your career, or bringing up kids. Other short-term events often seem more important than the long-time achievements. It is eminently important to celebrate results, small or big, as you go through them.

Start the exercise of **recognizing yourself.** Recognize not only what you have accomplished by now, but also **who you have become.**

 Exercise Tool 1: Recognize Your Accomplishments.

Answer the questions:

- What accomplishments did you have during the last ten years? Write them down year by year.
- What did you accomplish this month?
- What did you accomplish today?
- Who have you become during this process?
  (State new personality traits that you have attained during this process).

STEP 12 | BE PATIENT AND TRUST

 Write your answers into your **Brave Dreaming Journal**.

 Exercise Tool 2: How will you celebrate your accomplishments and yourself?
Look back at your manifestation plan of how you will celebrate your accomplishments. Go through every step in your plan and update and make changes according to your ongoing achievements.

Write down in your **Brave Dreaming Journal:**

- How will you celebrate what you have done?
- How will you celebrate who you have become?

Giving Thanks.

A way to give thanks to life is to remind yourself of all the wonder that happens without you controlling or changing it. It just happens.

When you see the perfection in the wholeness of nature, you can trust that there is a perfection about you as well. You are part of the whole; as nature is perfect, so are you. Like the beautiful colors in a simple flower, growing with perfection in nature, just there for you to enjoy it. You are as perfect as the flower.

STEP 12 | BE PATIENT AND TRUST

When you follow your dream, you are playing your perfect role in life, just like the flower. Life and nature are always moving into something more, which is our natural state as well. We are all striving to grow and evolve. The tree and the flower are growing into perfection with all their beauty, without trying to force things into happening. They just naturally grow into their perfection.

You are no different, and you are a part of nature, striving to expand into more. Learn from the flowers and the plants, trust that everything will unfold in a perfect way without pushing and struggling. **Accept what is and go with the flow.**

Start to give thanks for the small things you already have.

To give thanks is one of the most **powerful tools** you will be using. When you give thanks, you are telling the creative force that you appreciate what you have received, and naturally the force will try to give you more of what you appreciate. Start to give thanks to every small thing you have received and make it a habit of always looking for reasons to be thankful.

Yes! You have so much to be thankful for. Even if you have a physical disability, give thanks for what you have. Give thanks that you can see, walk, hear, and that you can smell and taste good food. Give thanks that you have friends, family and maybe kids.

Give thanks to nature. Look at the wonder around you and see the perfection in all. When you can see how life is so amazingly and perfectly put together in harmony, then you can trust that your dream somehow fits into it all.

"You are supposed to be here right now, doing what you are doing."

Every time you say thank you for something from your heart,
you know that you are in a positive flow with life.

Start to say thank you all day long for all things in life.

- **Give thanks to everybody that has crossed your path.**
  They brought you something, some experience (positive or negative), and they helped in shaping you, to become who you are right now. Remember, you are special and unique. Accept and love yourself as you are.

- **Give thanks to the hard times and good times in life.**
  The hard times usually teach us the greatest lessons. Nobody lives without experiencing both of these sides. Think about it from a different perspective: if you didn't have the hard times, you wouldn't be able to learn some valuable lessons allowing you to appreciate the good times even more.

- **Give thanks to all the past hurt and pain.**
  Not like you want it again, but because it took you into a new and different path of life.

- **Give thanks for all the wonderful times in your life.**
  Times that you enjoyed alone or together with someone special.

Most importantly of all, is to give thanks to YOURSELF for:

- Having the willingness to continue and not giving up.
- Valuing yourself enough.
- Being truthful to yourself.
- Knowing that you are worthy of your dream.
- Going through this manual to understand the process of creating your dream, and reminding yourself of your inner strength, beauty and truth.

Give yourself love and a big warm hug for creating your life intentionally, doing what you genuinely feel you came here to do, which is your life's purpose.

Give thanks to yourself for valuing yourself enough to live your dream.

Never give up on yourself!
Trust yourself and trust in life!

YES, YOU CAN!

Your toolbox for life. With the twelve creation steps, you now have a complete toolbox. You can apply these tools towards any dream during your entire life. Know that the steps can show up in a mixed order at any time. Follow your intuition to take action as they come. Trust, have patience, and remember to celebrate yourself and have fun.

Summary:

- You have recognized your accomplishments of what you have done and of whom you have become.
- You have understood the importance of celebrating each step on your path towards your dream.
- You know the power of giving thanks to yourself and all parts of life.
- You have a complete toolbox for life.

Summary Exercise Tools:

1. Recognize your accomplishments.
2. How will you celebrate your accomplishments and yourself?

What you have done so far:

Step 1: You have made your dream lab.
Step 2: You are becoming aware of your thoughts and feelings.
Step 3: You are defining your dream with unlimited time and money.
Step 4: You are finding your intention and what you believe or know about your dream.
Step 5: You made your manifestation plan to make your dream real faster.
Step 6: You are defining how you can send out your dream using your new dream statement.
Step 7: You are brainstorming where and how you can research about your dream.
Step 8: You are recognizing signs through using your inspiration, intuition, and synchronicity.
Step 9: You know when to take action on your dreams and that you can't fail, only fall.
Step 10: You are accepting what is in life, knowing that happiness and love is an inside job.
Step 11: You are understanding the importance of trust, patience and the perfection of life.
Step 12: You are celebrating what you have become and you are giving thanks to every part of life.

FINAL WORDS

We'd like to sincerely **THANK YOU** for coming this far on your journey. The knowledge and experience you now have for living intentionally and creating your dream is something that very few people know about.

Once you have embarked on this journey, there is no way back, as you will feel that you have learned something of truth that is different from anything you have previously known.

In the coming time, you will have great experiences, unlike anything that you had before. Some of your dreams will turn out entirely different than you expected, which usually is something much better than your original dream. Other dreams will take time, as there may be more that needs to be cleared before you can receive it.

When you are on this journey of awareness, you will have the ability to watch your life in a new way. It will be like standing beside yourself and watching what is going on. You will be able to watch your reactions, thoughts and feelings without getting involved in them.

Gaining a new awareness doesn't mean that life will be soft and smooth all the time. Actually, when you get a greater awareness, the first thing that happens is that you will become aware of the sides of yourself that you still haven't worked through. These are the sides that are holding you back from getting what you desire.

These imperfect parts of you are like programs running in the background and you are not aware of them. Slowly you will gain awareness. Only when you are aware of all your imperfect sides will you be able to have them go away from your life. When you shine a light into the darkness, the darkness disappears. Let everything bubble up and welcome it. Don't fight it.

Observe what is going on without any judgment,
and it will dissolve by itself.

Finally, remember that fulfillment and happiness in life is an inside job. Nothing in the outside world will create lasting happiness. Only when you find your peace and happiness inside can you have **everything outside** and live without attachment.

Please let us know how this knowledge has impacted your life. We would love to hear from you.

Lots of Love… until we see you again.

Mats & Maria Löfkvist

Founders, Global Mentor Aid
info@globalmentoraid.org
www.globalmentoraid.org

CPSIA information can be obtained
at www.ICGtesting.com
Printed in the USA
BVHW022028100419
545206BV00010B/48/P